RESOLVING
THE RACE ISSUE
IN AMERICA

RESOLVING
THE RACE ISSUE
IN AMERICA

Living Beyond Race

Charles Williams

Published in 2009 by
Parenting Institute of America Inc.
P.O. Box 1102
Lilburn, GA. 30048

Resolving the Race Issue in America
Edited by Rekha Vasudeva
Includes bibliographical references and index.

Library of Congress Catalogue Number TX: 4704794

ISBN: 978-0-9772579-4-2

To Sudie Tucker Kincaid

Acknowledgments

This book was made possible by the kind contributions of Joyce Johnson Boggess, Renée Flanagan Karriem, Angela Releford, Rekha Vasudeva, and staff at the Auburn Street Library in Atlanta, GA. Without the help of these gifted individuals this work would have not been completed.

The person I am most indebted to is my mother, a woman who supported me in all of my endeavors. It is to her that I dedicate this book.

OUR MOTHER OF HUMARIA

Sudie Tucker Kincaid
1928 - 2008

OUR FATHER OF HUMARIA

Waightstill Tucker
1896 - 1984

Necro!

Punic War

The First Negro

Preface

When identity is assumed before truth can be analyzed, the search for truth is abandoned. Identity then becomes truth, and its preservation becomes the purpose of life. Existence is viewed through the eyes of identity, not through the eyes of truth.

Three qualities influence our perception of existence: virtue, passion, and ignorance. It is from these qualities that the seeds of identity are generated. The seed born of the desire for dominance is conceived from the quality of ignorance. The seed born of the desire for liberation is conceived from the quality of passion. The seed born of the desire for harmony is conceived from the quality of virtue. These different seeds of identity are sown throughout human society by three schools of thought: groupism, individualism, and humanism. Of the three schools that disseminate identity, groupism exerts the greatest influence. Ninety percent of the human population extracts its identity from a group. Of the remaining ten percent, sixty percent identify as individuals and forty percent identify with humanity. This composition of identity has existed for 5,000 years, since the rise of western civilization. The groupist insurgence that coincided with this period gave birth to the age of dissension and incited the quest for human domination.

At no time in history have greater efforts been made to stifle human intellect and suppress creativity. The result has diminished humanity in both stature and vision. In the era before the groupist reign, a person's greatest quest was to discover his humanity. During the golden age of civility, creativity and intellect were the forces that propelled human society. The great works of art and philosophy produced in this age have never been replicated. These great achievements were all made possible by the vision of a unified humanity, a dynamic that's been missing in society for 5,000 years. Groupism destroyed the vision of unity by accentuating the divergence rather than the similarities of mankind. The groupist ideal prevails because of the oppressive nature in which it is disseminated. The seed of groupist identity is planted early in childhood, before it can be resisted. Sowing the seed early in life makes it possible to destroy a child's humanity before the perception of truth develops. The groupist concept of identity is created by the seeds of fear. For most human beings, fear is the first emotion. Inciting fear by arousing suspicion stirs apprehension about things that appear to be different.

Using this process, human beings can create identity using the things they are taught to fear. The greatest fear for groupists is that which does not reflect them. Those who don't mirror them are classified as "other." Groupist identity must be dualistic; it requires at least two components. An object of contention must be invented, such as race or sex, which provides the catalyst for creating these two identities. One identity is dominant; the other identity is collateral.

The dominant identity is created by usurping power and fearing insurrection. The collateral identity is created by apathy. Those invested with the power of dominance use it as the impetus to preserve their identity. To do this, they create receptor offspring for the transfer of power. The subordinate class has no incentive to preserve its identity and thus makes no conscious effort to do so. Collateral identity is not transferred during childhood because there is no conscious desire to create it. Its existence is purely incidental.

The process of disseminating groupist identity is clearly illustrated by blacks and whites. Dominant white identity is assigned by parents before the age of five. The impetus behind assigning this identity is the preservation of power. Collateral black identity is never assigned by parents because of the stigma assigned to it. How could anyone justify bringing a child into what they perceive as a world of oppression? They offer no explanation for not assigning identity because there is no conscious intent to create it. Black parents avoid assigning collateral identity; instead they allow society to assign it for them.

A father's power to assign identity establishes ancestral order. Evoking this life-changing power is akin to inducing second birth, the birth of identity. Black fathers never exercise this power. They allow strangers or those barely known to their children to exercise it for them. This reluctance keeps their children mired in groupist existence.

Accepting collateral identity subjects one to oppression. Oppression is the fuel that drives the engine of the second school of identity, individualism. However, individualism assigns no identity to the oppressor; its perception of identity is of a singular nature. It only identifies with features unique to the individual. Those characteristics have no physical point of reference such as sex or race; they exist only in the realm of cognition.

Individual identity, unlike groupist identity, cannot be induced by fear and cannot be assigned. It must be realized through individual experience. Its outward manifestation can be observed as a quest for knowledge that leads to liberation. Humanist identity, taught by the third school, is also manifested singularly. It makes no allowance for the separatism created by race, gender, religion, nationality, ethnicity or individuality. Its broad spectrum embodies the oneness of humanity.

The seeds of humanist identity are generated by compassion and are sown by those who possess soft hearts. Groupism and individualism harden the hearts of their proponents by imposing isolation. Love exists only for members of the group or for the individual. The expression of love is tendered by a set criterion. Humanistic love has no conditions; it seeks to love only for love's sake. Love is the driving principle.

Humanism, like groupism, is often introduced during childhood but is effective only when the surrounding environment is able to support it. It flounders in an atmosphere of selfishness and fear. Selfishness and fear harden the heart and inhibit the flow of compassion. Love has no greater enemy than fear. For true love to exist, it must be fearless. It cannot have boundaries, conditions, or limits. This type of love is the embodiment of humanism.

All sentient beings that enter this world undergo some form of conditioning. The most critical form of conditioning is that which establishes a person's identity. The administration of this conditioning is conducted by parents who have been in some way influenced by these three schools of thought. Studying these three institutions can provide insight into the origin of identity and help one overcome the limitations they impose.

There are basically two types of people in this world: those who erect illusions and those who dismantle them. One of the greatest illusions ever erected is race. In America there are more people erecting this illusion than there are dismantling it. As a result, you find millions of people living the illusion of race. Erecting the illusion is much easier than dismantling it. To dismantle it requires an act of God.

In my life I have been quite fortunate. I have never fallen into the illusion of race. I have always identified with the space inside my family circle. I owe my great fortune to my Grandfather and his daughter, the beautiful woman who gave birth to me. My mother, Sudie Tucker Kincaid, was not one to erect illusions. She never yielded to the allurement of race. She lived her life beyond race and she shared that life with everyone she knew. Living beyond race allowed her to live inside others.

It is because she is living inside me that I have been inspired to write this book. It is to the life that she lived that I pay tribute. My hope is that by speaking through me she will come to live inside you.

About the Author

Charles **Williams** is a native of Western North Carolina. He is an author, philosopher, entrepreneur, and father of six children. He became interested in family advocacy in 1993, after his son and daughter were convicted of crimes and sentenced to time in prison. Viewing their imprisonment as his own personal failure, he began an extensive self-examination. The goal was to acquire the deepest understanding of fatherhood.

This quest for truth lasted four years and involved thousands of people. It led to the establishment of Save the Family Institute (STFI), a Georgia nonprofit 501(c)(3) organization that conducts family research and development. STFI collects and analyzes data on American families to determine the family's fitness in the areas of health, leadership, formation, identity, organization, and spirituality. The primary focus is the extended family, all of the bloodline nuclear families combined. STFI believes that a unified extended family creates the best environment for human growth and development. STFI provides a platform for family advocacy to all sober minded people who love the family, regardless of race, religion, ethnicity, nationality, culture, and politics.

Table of Contents

About the Introduction

The introduction to this book is an excerpt from a paper presented during a conference at Morehouse College in Atlanta, GA on August 30th, 2007. The theme of the conference was "Celebrating Our Ancestors." This paper, entitled "Let the Negro Die," was chosen to introduce this book because it helps to create the mindset needed to dismantle race. This introduction contains vital information that can be used in the struggle to free the American people from the bondage of race.

Introduction

"Let the Negro Die"

The theme of this conference is "Celebrating Ancestors." With this in mind I think it's ir that we understand what is being celebrated. '

our ancestors is not celebrating race. Identifying them racially is an insult. Our ancestors had no racial identity. They identified with God, family, tribe, culture, people, and nation. Every attempt to impose race on them was rejected. So why, then, do we try to do it? Is it the Negro in us? Are we so vain that we have to stoop to that level? Must we bring our ancestors down in order to lift ourselves up? They did not embrace Negro identity. Insinuating otherwise does not honor them; in fact it demeans them. The celebration of our ancestors is not a celebration of the Negro.

Negro identity was born from a stigmatic projection that first appeared in the minds of Europeans. There was no term used by our ancestors that referred to a Negro race. The concept was completely foreign.[1]

The terms Nubian, Egyptian, Ethiopian, Yoruba, Ashanti, Ibo, and Kermit have no racial supposition. These terms identify people who share a common culture, not race. No inference was ever made that suggests that all Africans were Nubian, Egyptian, Ethiopian, Yoruba, Ashanti, Ibo, or Kermit. Before the term Negro was uttered, there had been no reference to a black race by Africans. There is no history of a homogeneous African people.

The concept of a Negro race as an entity unto itself is not African in origin. There has never been a time in African history where people came together to form a black race. If there were indeed a sense of a unified black race in Africa, colonization would have never been possible. No effort was ever made by African people to unify as a race to dominate whites. No attempt has ever been made by a black race to subjugate a white race. This precept originated with Europeans. Before the first Negroes appeared in the

BIMBA   NUBIAN   FULANI   OBA

EGYPTIAN   ETHIOPIAN   FON

IBO   MANDINKA   MENDE   MALINDI

NUPE   MALI   ASHANTI

MOOR   WOLOF   YORUBA   ZULU

EDO   BERBER   JOLOF

OYO   MANDINGO   DYULA   KERMIT

1740s there were no avowed representatives of the so-called black race. No one represented the race because in the minds of the ancestors race was nonexistent. With this understood, it was only logical to conclude that any attempt that we made to impose race on them would be soundly rejected. They found no reason to embrace the identity of the walking dead.

It took 2,000 years to produce a Negro. One of the earliest attempts was made by the Romans in 265 BC. The Romans were among the first people to use a term referring to color to identify Africans. The incident occurred on a battlefield during the first Punic War.

According to my Grandfather who relayed this story to me as a young boy, Roman legions were engaged in fierce combat with Phoenician warriors. The Phoenicians employed Numidians, African mercenaries to help them defend the ancient city of Carthage.[2] These Roman warriors had never had contact with a live human being with dark skin. Their only contact with dark skin occurred after one of their Roman brethren died. When someone with fair skin dies, the skin turns black. Because this was the experience of the Romans, their first response to Africans was fear. They feared they were fighting the "Walking Dead."

One of my Grandfather's favorite pastimes was telling war stories like this. His favorite war story was about how his unit defeated the Germans without ever firing a shot. While on patrol with Company "C" of the 808 Pioneer Infantry in the Meuse-Argonne Woods in France his unit was attacked by Germans who after seeing them ran away without firing a shot. No one could explain why, they ran.

Sometime later, word came down that the reason they fled was because they thought they were fighting dead men. Company "C" was all black and the Germans had never seen black people before. They thought that the men of Company "C" were the corpses of white soldiers that had already been killed and had come back to life. Knowing that you cannot kill someone who is already dead the Germans ran away in fear.

The fact is, there were no walking dead; it was only an illusion. The fascination with this illusion gave birth to Negro identity. In the minds of the Romans the African was the color of death. The term used to identify these "Walking Dead" was "Necro."[3] "Necro" is a shorten version of Necrosis, a Latin term that refers to a decaying body. Negro is a derivative of Necrosis.

The term "Necro" used in this instance did not identify race. Romans, like Africans, had no concept of race. They identified people according to region, culture, tribe, and nation. People of African descent who adopted Roman culture and customs were also identified as Romans. After invading Africa in 1419, the Portuguese also used the term Negro. Their use of the term was a continuation of the practice started by the Romans. Portuguese, like Romans, does not identify race. Portuguese identifies a culture and nation. After the Spanish arrived in Africa they also used the term Negro, but like the Romans and the Portuguese the term was not used in a racial context. Spanish, like Portuguese and Roman, is not a racial designation; it identifies a culture and nation.

The British arrived in Africa in 1530 and they too used the term Negro to identify Africans. The British use of the term, however, was different. The first British encounter with an African was similar to that of the Romans. William Hawkins and his crew had never seen a live human being with dark skin.[4] Like the Romans, they thought they were viewing the "Walking Dead." Because race was a component of their identity, their use of the term Negro was to identify race. The British were the first people to identify people by race. It was during the reign of King Edward I that the British discovered what they referred to as the super, excellent quality of white skin.[5] Enamored by their new discovery, they introduced the practice of viewing life through the veil of skin.

White skin, they enjoined, was the quintessence of all physical attributes. So much so, that it was deified and made the standard by which all human beauty was to be judged. According to pragmatists, the opulent nature of white skin was most elegantly displayed by British royalty, the majesty of which took on literary form in the Metrical Romances, Chronicles and Legends of the 13th, 14th, and 15th Centuries. This literature was the first ever written that expressed what the British recognized as the exuberant qualities of whiteness.

Whiteness associated with royalty was thought to mean liberation for rich and poor alike. For the lower classes, connecting with royalty was as simple as taking pride in one's skin. This social phenomenon that changed the course of history by altering human perception was not sparked by exposure to dark skin. There were no blacks residing in Britain during the 13th Century. Whiteness had been ensconced as the standard of beauty in Britain for 300 years before William Hawkins discovered blacks during his legendary cruise to Guinea in 1530.[6] No blacks had resided in Britain since 210 AD when a "Division of

African Moors" was sent to Britain by Rome to defend Hadrian's Wall. Their occupation ended shortly when the Romans pulled back their forces from "Britannia," as it was known in those days.[7]

Even though there were no blacks present in the Kingdom, whiteness carried extraordinary significance. It reached its pinnacle while Queen Elizabeth I, known adorably as the "Alabaster Queen," was on the throne. Elizabeth, in an effort to portray herself as a symbol of purity, took whiteness to a new level. Jilted by her married lover who refused to divorce his wife and marry her, Elisabeth was outraged. To cover her shame and humiliation, she put forth an image of purity.

Elizabeth was naturally pale, but like many ladies then and since she freshened her "lilies" at the cosmetic table. In "Partheniads" written by George Puttenham in 1579 there is this charming description of the queen the English Nation adored:

> **Her cheeke, her chinne, her neck, her nose**
> **This was a lillye, that was a rose;**
> **Her hande so white as whales bone,**
> **Her finger tipt with cassidone;**
> **Her bosome, sleeke as Paris plaster**
> **Held up two bowles of Alabaster.**

Nowhere in the world has whiteness been celebrated with more pomp and circumstance than in Merry Ol' England. Even the great William Shakespeare found the combination of the lily and the rose irresistible. He wrote these celebrated words in recognition:

> **'Tis beauty truly blent, whose red and white**
> **Nature's own sweet and cunning hand laid on.**

The British discovery of blackness in Africa was thought to confirm all of their racial supposition.

When someone assumes racial identity, a psychological barrier is erected that obstructs free association. Having assumed a racial posture the British could not share their humanity with the Africans. Infested with this racial animus, the British led a crusade in Africa to produce Negroes. Every conceivable form of coercion was used, but not one native-born African came forward to identify him or herself as a Negro. No one could, there was no Negro model to emulate. No African had ever lived the life of a Negro. To live the Negro life the African would have to live within a space that was controlled and operated exclusively by whites. This space could only be created outside of the tribal circle. It could not be created in Africa because Africans lived inside the circle. No attempt had been made by Africans to live external lives outside of the tribal circle. The customs and traditions of the family and tribe guided and connected them internally. The British could not see this internal connection; they could only see externals. The great civilization that Africans built internally was not visible to them.

To become a Negro the African would have to give up internal life. The customs and traditions of family and tribe would have to be abandoned. With no customs or traditions to guide them, Africans would have become from the internal perspective walking dead. This was in fact what the British wanted to create, a people who had no internal life, people who were controlled exclusively by externals.

Undeterred by the failed attempts of the British to create a Negro, the American white male took up the task in the late 1600s. One of the first steps taken was to give the term Negro legitimacy. On all deeds, wills, court records, warrants, titles, and shipping records, Africans were identified as Negroes. Using the term on legal documents created a legal entity that was recognized by the courts. According to the precedent set, all Africans were Negroes regardless of their ethnic background.[8] Even though the court agreed that all Africans were Negroes, the court had no power to infuse Negro identity. The African was a Negro in the eyes of the court but that perception did not translate into actual acceptance by the Africans themselves. A second step was required.

That second step was to establish a culture of racial privilege. Laws were enacted that granted and denied privileges on the basis of race. Among these laws was a law legalizing slavery. With its passage African identity came under a blistering assault. All tribal symbols, ornaments, instruments, and rituals were done away with. Every conceivable form of brutality was employed to create a space to break the African spirit, but members of the Fon, Yoruba, Ibo, Fanti, Ashanti, Mandingo, and Jolof were unrelenting. They refused to abandon their African identity to become Negroes.

The First Negro

After all else failed, to give life to the fiendish caricature dwelling in his mind, the American white male fathered the Negro. The first people to identify themselves as

Negroes were mulattos.[9] The fathers were white males and the mothers were African slaves. The first Negroes were not born in Africa; they were born in America in the 1740s. These people had no God, family, tribe, people, culture, or nation of their own. Rejected by the Anglo and the African, the first avowed representatives of the Negro race were outcast. With no lineal or cultural connection, race was their only asset, and race was what they passed on to their offspring.

Since appearing in the 1740s, there has been an ongoing struggle to keep Negro identity alive. The white male has been the biggest contributor. From the white male the Negro learned the principles of race. Race, for the white male was the beginning, middle, and end of all things. Race, the Negro was taught, hovered high above family, friends, nation, people, culture, and even God. Protecting, honoring, defending, and advancing the race was the noblest of all undertakings. For the race one should be prepared to kill, steal, maim, deceive, kidnap, torture, rape, enslave, and die, if need be. Nothing is more precious than race. Race is the essence of your being. Nothing exists beyond race and the race above all races is the white race. Selling race, the white male exercised the greatest influence on Negro identity. It was on the foundation of race that Negro identity was built.

The most outspoken critic of the Negro was the African. From the African perspective, the Negro was walking dead. He had no God, family, tribe, people, culture, or nation he could claim. His life was one-dimensional. The only thing the Negro could claim as his own was race. Race for the African was a death trap. To embrace it was to submit to racial domination. No Negro existed until someone claimed the bottom position. The ancestors were not at the bottom; they did not look up to the white male, they looked down on him. The white male, like the Negro, was considered walking dead; both viewed life from an external perspective.

From the Negro perspective the African was just another Negro. The two could not connect because the African was thought to be less intelligent. It is ironic that the white male had also come to the same conclusion. Negroes were more civil than Africans. They made better slaves, were more congenial, and less apt to run away.[10] They loved their masters and did not desert them in their hour of need.

Having witnessed the show of such sentiments, the African was outraged and a rift developed with the Negro. The African wanted freedom while the Negro wanted to please. For the Negro, pleasing his master proved his superior intellect because it won him favor over the African. Shown favor by the master was interpreted as a license to abuse the African. For responding to the abuse inflicted by the Negro, the African was ostracized. Everything African was rejected.[11] The African was given no role to play in keeping Negro identity alive. With no input from Africans, attention shifted to the white male.

The white male had to be given a major role. After all, he created the Negro. Could it be that the best way to keep the identity alive was to imitate the white man? That's exactly what the Negro did. Everything African was replaced with everything American. By imitating the white male, Negro identity was energized. This energized form of Negro identity became known as Negritude.

Negritude emerged in the 1860s, and for the first time a beleaguered, battered and broken people, who walked with their backs slumped and their heads bowed, began to walk upright. They were inspired by their faith that the blight that had befallen them could be removed. Their hopes were partially realized in the form of emancipation, civil rights, and integration. Although a long time coming, these hard-fought victories appeared to have stemmed the tide. They were living proof of what the Negro could do if he imitated the white man. The credit, however, was not given to the white man; it was given to Negritude, which was loosely defined as Negro pride. Negritude demanded a change of attitude; it was championed by Fredrick Douglas, Harriet Tubman, W.E.B. Dubois, George Washington Carver, Marcus Garvey, Malcolm X, and Martin Luther King, all of whom identified themselves as Negroes.

Externally, Negritude lived up to its billing; it produced a Supreme Court Justice, Secretary of State, National Security Adviser, Cabinet Members, CEOs of major corporations, stardom, fancy clothes, cars, homes, yachts, and a per capita income that surpassed any third world country. What Negritude failed to do, however, was to restore the humanity of the people. The goal of Negritude was to improve the external image; it did not address the more serious issue of how we interact with one another. The deficit has always been character. Constructing some elaborate façade behind which to hide does not build character.

Decorating the tree of life will never restore its value. Human life in black society has less value today than it did during slavery. In 2004 there were an estimated 400,000 children born to African American mothers. In the same year there were some 160,000 abortions. Of the 400,000 children that survived the womb, seventy percent were born out of wedlock. And of this seventy percent, thirty-five percent could not identify their biological father.

African Americans, the latest incarnation of the Negro, have some of the highest rates of HIV infection, incarceration, single parenthood, obesity, high school dropouts, and divorce in America. Black on black crime, suicide, alcohol and drug abuse, moral decadence and apathy are running rampant in black society. Nothing to date has been able to stop what some describe as a self-inflicted holocaust. Negritude, the 135 year old initiative to liberate Black America, has been a success externally but internally it has been a dismal failure. Emancipation, integration, civil rights, affirmative action, higher education, athletics, entertainment stardom, high public office, four trillion dollars in government subsidized food, housing, and medical assistance, and numerous other programs have not stopped the bleeding. The bleeding is internal and no external arrangement, no matter how elaborate, can stop it. What has to be dealt with is internal dysfunction. The problem is much deeper than freedom of opportunity, justice, and economic deprivation—these things are only ancillary. The root problem is a defective identity and no amount of freedom, justice, money, or religion can fix it. What value are wealth, freedom, and justice when your identity is holding you hostage?

The struggle being waged by the new Negro, the African American is no different than the struggle waged by the old Negro. Nothing has changed except the name attached to the identity. Negro, colored, black, African American, people of color, the name is not the issue. At issue is what the name identifies. The name identifies a position at the bottom. Maintaining an identity that positions you at the bottom is not a great accomplishment. The Negro was invented to facilitate racial domination. Someone had to claim the bottom position. That position belongs to the Negro; he claimed it. Struggling to keep the identity alive will never change its position. The Negro will always be looking up at the white man because his identity positions him at the bottom.

Although positioned at the bottom, the Negro likes to boast of his greatness. "The Negro is the original man," he claims. "The white man came from the Negro. The Negro built the Pyramids. Negroes were great Kings and Queens. The Negro was the first mathematician, the first scientist," on, and on, and on. All of which is sheer fantasy because there were no Negroes until the 1740s. If these Negroes who profess to be greater than the white man were put in the white man's position, how long could they maintain it? How effective would they be in the position of the oppressor? Could they convince whites to accept the bottom position? How far would they go to keep the whites down? Would they lynch them? Could they do to whites what was done to their ancestors? How far would the Negro go to stay on top?

Sometimes the white male is conflicted in his role as the "top man." Being the oppressor is no fun. There is no pleasure in being forced to keep someone beneath you, which he must do to maintain his power. Although he is the greatest proponent of racial domination, the white male has also been its greatest opponent. Without his support the Negro would still be enslaved. Freeing the Negro is commendable but it has not eliminated racial domination.

No one can deny its existence. Racial domination built this country. Today's white male did not have to earn this power; it was given to him. He did not have to kill, steal, maim, deceive, kidnap, torture, rape, enslave, or die to get it. It was a gift from the Founding Fathers.

James Monroe   **Thomas Jefferson**   **James Madison**

They did what was necessary to amass this power. To preserve their legacy, today's white male must maintain this power. He has no choice; he is tied to a tradition of dominance. Being a white male in America has no meaning if you cannot dominate racially. And domination is made easier when there are those who feel obliged to accept the bottom position. The bottom position and the top position are social constructs that divide humanity. The terms used to identify these positions, fixes the focus of identity on externals, which minimizes the value of human life.

The question you must ask yourself is, why embrace something external that binds you internally? Those who do so have no internal life. They have no concept of who they are internally. They live their lives outside of themselves. Because they only pursue external life, all of their activities are external. Everything flows from the outside in. Nothing flows from the inside out. With no internal directive, they cannot pursue an internal objective. Yielding only to external influences, the control of their lives is taken from them.

External life, be it black or white, is a non-lethal form of death. Human beings show life only when stimulated externally. The Negro ancestors did not submit to external control, they lived their lives internally. They were guided from within by the customs and traditions developed by their ancestors. Because they were not controlled externally they were never attracted to Negro identity. Race could not bridge the chasm that separated the Negro and the African. They saw no value in keeping dead men alive.

Keeping the Negro alive has been a costly affair. The investment in time, energy, and capital is enormous. Billions of dollars are spent each year just to maintain a façade. The current return on this investment is the highest rates of out of wedlock births, child abandonment, abortion, drug addiction, crime, incarceration, divorce, single parenthood, spousal abuse, child abuse, and sexual molestation found anywhere in the civilized world.

The Negro struggle will never be won. The wrong battle is being fought on the wrong battlefield. Doing for the race is not doing for self. The real self is not who a person appears to be externally. The real self is the inner being who cannot be identified racially. The inner being derives its identity from family. We turn to race when our family has no identity. Family competes with race for sovereignty over its members. When the family becomes race, the family loses its individuality. It cannot regulate itself because it has no life of its own. With no customs or traditions to guide it from within, the family is left vulnerable to external control. When race takes control, family ceases to exist. The family is sacrificed to maintain the identity of the race. Taking the family back from the race is where the real battle must take place. Victory on this battlefield will guarantee liberation. Each family must take up this internal struggle. Traditions and customs must be developed that guide the family internally. Honoring these customs and traditions will empower the family to create its own identity.

The external struggle is not the family struggle. The external struggle takes place outside of the family. It is only a distraction, a game that no one wins. The white male is not the winner. There are no winners in the skin game we call race. Everyone who plays the game is a loser. The white male may have all of the toys at the end of the day but he doesn't have peace. Anyone who allows race to usurp the family will never find peace. With no peace there is no happiness. Real happiness cannot be arranged externally; it can only be pursued internally. The struggle for happiness must originate inside. Those who have embraced Negro identity have been duped and must come to grips with this reality.

Negro identity is a psychological straightjacket that binds you internally. The ancestors, knowing this, rejected the identity. In terms of content, the white male has contributed more to Negro identity than anyone else. For this he takes no credit. To avoid being implicated, the white male has convinced the Negro that he has always existed, that he is in fact a product of his own invention.

No people left to their own devices would have ever become Negroes. The Negro's psychology and tongue are not his own. He thinks with the mind and speaks with the tongue of the white man. Having rejected the customs and traditions of his ancestors, the Negro is but the shadow of the white male. Because he is not his own person, everywhere the Negro appears he wreaks havoc. The invasion of Africa is a prime example.

Joseph Roberts

Jane Roberts

Joseph Cheeseman

Beverly Yates

James Payne

Alfred Russell

Of all of the invaders, the American Negro has inflicted more damage on African Culture than any other. Influenced by the American Negro, the African has become a Negro. American Negroes, who have taken leadership positions, as was the case in Liberia, have done great harm to African Civilization. They have destroyed the internal institutions of custom and tradition and replaced them with western decadence and immorality. Understanding this, how can we in all honesty come before our ancestors as Negroes? We show them no honor in doing so. Negro identity is an abomination created to impute mediocrity. Rejected by our ancestors, this humiliating concoction commands no respect, only pity. Because they have turned their backs on their ancestors, those who live this life have been cursed. In keeping Negro identity alive they do a great disservice, not only to their ancestors but also to humanity at large.

For the Negro the best way to celebrate the ancestors is to give up external identity. Negro identity has severed the connection with the ancestors. To reconnect, Negro identity must be abandoned. Nothing would please the ancestors more. Pulling the plug on Negro identity is the key to liberation. To begin this process, we must take the family back from the race. Race is not all that we can be. There is life beyond race; our ancestors lived it. Everyone can live this life if we adopt customs and traditions that guide us from within. Thank You!

End Notes
Introduction

(1) Na'im Akbar, Ph.D., The Creation of the Negro, from the paper "African Roots of Black Personality", *Akbar Papers in African Psychology*, 99–104.

(2) Na'im Akbar, The Creation of the Negro, [online] 2004 mindpro. com/documents.

(3) John Gibson Warry, Warfare in the Classical World (Baltimore: Salamander Books Ltd., 1980).

(4) Akbar, 99–104.

(5) Richard Hakluyt, The Principal Navigations, Voyages, Traffiques and Discoveries of the English Nation (New York: Macmillan, 1589).

(6) Walter Clyde Curry, The Middle English Ideal of Personal Beauty (Baltimore: J. H. Furst, 1916) 80–98.

(7) Hakluyt.

(8) John Hodgson, History of Northumberland [online] 1840, www. archive.org

(8) F. James Davis, Who is Black? One Nation's Definition (University Park: Pennsylvania State Univ. Press, 1991).

(9) Stephan Talty, Mulatto America: At the Crossroads of Black and White Culture (New York: Harper Collins, 2003).

(10) Gad J. Heuman and James Walvin, The Slavery Reader (New York: Routledge, 2003).

(11) Harold Issacs, "The American Negro and Africa: Some Notes," The Phylon Quarterly [online] 1959 www.jstor.org/pss/273045

PART ONE

Living External life

1

The First Nation of the Race

There are numerous myths about race being propagated in American society today. One of the most common among them is the idea that people have been living for the race as long as the physical characteristics that define race have been known. Race is a notoriously nebulous concept. Before a physical property can be scientifically examined, it must be objectively defined so that accurate measurements of variables can be made. Defining race has been based on subjective taxonomic classification, morphological interpretation, and physiognomic characteristics, exercises that are frighteningly akin to phrenology. Race has yet to be defined in objective genetic terms that are quantifiably

3

measurable, rendering attempts at truly scientific discussion hopelessly futile.[1] Even though the physical traits chosen to identify race have always existed, their application as a means of assigning human identity is a relatively new practice.

No people in ancient times were so culturally void that they had to rely on physical traits for identity.[2] Assigning human identity according to physical characteristics such as skin, hair, and eye color or any other physical feature was uncalled for because people lived internal lives. The customs and traditions passed down by their ancestors guided them from within. There were no terms used to identify them externally or dictate behavior. People lived to please their ancestors not to please the race.

Socrates, the father of western philosophy, valued who he was internally, more so than who he was externally.[3] When approached by adversaries who imprisoned him and sentenced him to death, he responded by mocking them. He told them, "You can't kill me, you can't even see me, all you see is my shadow." The shadow he referred to was his body.

Socrates did not know himself as a body. He knew that his body was composed of atoms; these atoms had always existed, they existed before his body was formed. They previously composed other bodies and would reappear after his demise. Atoms that form white bodies reappear in black bodies after death and vise versa. Socrates knew himself to be that which was unchanging, not that which is constantly in flux. Knowing this he had no fear of death. To deny his enemies the notoriety of claiming that they had killed him Socrates, committed suicide by drinking poison.

None of the architects of western civilization such as Abraham, Moses, Plato, Aristotle, Alexander the Great, or Augustine identified themselves according to external attributes such as skin color. They lived internal lives. They were guided from within by the customs and traditions handed down by their ancestors. The foundations on which western and eastern civilization were built was internal. No one in ancient times lived external life.

External life is the life you live according to the dictates of race. The behavior that race dictates is based on what is perceived as the other race. This interaction between two or more races is external life. Those who live external lives, live for the race. They surrender their body, mind, and spirit to the race. Because race is the only life they know; they have no internal life.

For those who have no internal life, race is the beginning, middle, and end of all things. It hovers above family, friends, nation, people, culture, and even God. For the "Internally Dead," protecting, honoring, defending, and advancing the race is the noblest of all undertakings. For the race, the "Internally Dead" have been known to kill, steal, maim, kidnap, torture, rape, enslave, and die, if need be. They eat, sleep and breathe race. In their minds nothing exists beyond race. Every thought, every deed, every sound, every emotion, every dream, and every desire is racial. No one lives outside of the parameters of race and the race that is above all races is the white race.

These sentiments created the world's first external civilization. The architects were radical men, who, for the sake of acquiring power, severed ties with family heritage and ethnicity, leaving them bereft of cultural identity. Everything internal was lost. To fill the vacuum that was created, they chose race as their deliverer.

British Culture and Race

Race was first introduced by the British, who never mastered the art of living for the race. The rigidness of British culture would not allow it. There are elements of British culture that run deeper than race; these elements existed long before whiteness was introduced.[4] If forced to choose between living for the race and living for the family, the British would chose family.

Although whiteness was celebrated with great pomp and circumstance, replacing the family with race was unthinkable. Even though the concept of race was introduced in Britain, prior to the 1300s family was the primary source of British identity. The customs and traditions of the family played the greatest role in determining individual identity.

The quest for identity took place internally. No external identifier was required because identity flowed from the inside out, not from the outside in. This outward flow of identity was driven by family customs and traditions. These customs and traditions addressed every aspect of human life and guided the family from within. Members who strictly followed them were shielded from outside influences.

Race was an outside influence that did not belong to the family; the family belonged to the race. Claiming race opened the family up to intrusion by members of the lower classes. The class structure in British society was very stringent. Although race was shared, class was not. Distinctions were made. The class a person belonged to was not determined by his race; it was determined by his family of origin. He lived for the pleasure of his family, not for the pleasure of the race. Preserving the stature of British aristocracy was a family function that had nothing to do with race. This was done by utilizing the influence and resources of the family. According to British tradition, greatness was bestowed upon a person by his family not by his race.

The British family that was held in the highest esteem was the royal family. The sovereignty of the nation was never awarded to the race; it was awarded to a family. Even though Britain was the birthplace of race, attempts to make race the dominant identity failed because of the power and influence of the royal family. Queen Elizabeth was known as the "Alabaster Queen," but she was better known as the daughter of Henry VIII. Her family was held in higher esteem than her race. It was the influence of her family, not her race, which put her on the throne.

Not only did the queen benefit from being a member of the Tudor family, other members benefited as well. Titled gentry who governed the land, such as dukes, barons, earls, governors and others, came from family ranks. Before the concept of race was introduced, mankind relied most heavily on family and culture for identity. The first identities of record were derived from family relationships. Son and daughter of such and such, mother and father of such and such, sister and brother of such and such, and so on.

Even though race was held in high esteem in Britain, it did not replace family. The royal family's influence and power kept family in the forefront of the nation's consciousness. The king may have been a tyrant but his family had the power to subdue him. To address their grievances, the citizenry would often go to members of the royal family for relief. The king had to answer to the family. The family brought balance to the kingship. Being out of favor with the family has brought down many kings. In Britain race had to compete with family for dominance and there were other challenges as well.

Although viewing human life through a veil of skin was introduced in Britain, not everyone derived social and economic benefit from the practice. The prominence that whiteness attained was a result of being associated with royalty, and the social, political, and economic benefits that accrued were unavailable to the lower classes.

British commoners also had white skin but their social and economic status was unchanged by the miraculous discovery of whiteness. For the peasant, whiteness did not translate into social or economic gain. In fact it was quite the opposite. From 1553 to 1600 Britain was flooded with African emigrants brought in as indentured servants. These workers were taught British customs and trades. They worked for a period of five years to pay for their apprenticeship and were then given an opportunity to enter the job market. Because they worked for lower wages, their expertise as tradesmen was viewed as a threat by the white working class. In 1601 riots erupted in retaliation to African emigrants taking jobs from the lower classes. To end the violence, Queen Elizabeth I enacted the Deportation Act of 1601, which authorized the deportation of Britain's entire African population.

The societal structure in Britain only accommodated two classes, upper and lower. The aristocratic blue bloods composed the upper class, while the peasantry composed the lower class. Africans came in as members of the lower class and were accorded the same rights and privileges as the other members. No third tier composed exclusively of Africans was created to pacify the peasants. To create a third tier, laws were required that restricted access to goods, services, housing, employment, and equal protection under the law based on one's race. Even though Africans were an isolated minority in Britain, discrimination in the form of social and economic deprivation mandated by law never occurred. No laws were enacted that granted or denied privileges based solely on race.

Before the Races were Formed

When the first twenty Africans arrived at Jamestown, Virginia, in 1619, slavery did not exist in the British colonies. Contrary to popular myth, slavery did not become law the moment Africans landed in America. There were no oppressive laws passed quickly to satisfy greedy landowners who were lusting for power. Slavery was introduced gradually, one person at a time, one law at a time, and one colony at a time.[5] Before the advent of slavery there was no racial strife in America. Because of the severity of the elements, people of all races were forced to work together just to survive.

The period from 1620 to 1640 in terms of race relations could well be described as the Golden Age. At no time since have people of different races lived a freer and more peaceful life together.[6] In the Golden Age people did not identify with race. The British and Africans that composed the working class identified with their culture. Because the noble class relied so heavily on labor, the working class was treated with dignity and respect. No effort was made to divide people along racial lines; all were indentured servants, not slaves. During their tenure, servants were provided food and housing. African and British men and women worked side-by-side in the house and in the fields. Any African or British servant who broke the servant contract was punished equally. After serving their tenure of servitude, the British and the African became free men and were given what were known as "freedom dues," which consisted of a piece of land, some supplies, and a firearm.

In the late sixteenth century, the focus of the British economy shifted to accommodate expansion. New companies were created to set up colonies all over the world. To provide labor for the colonies, members of the working class were recruited for the labor force overseas and people who could not afford passage were hired as indentured servants. The indentured servant class did not consist entirely of unskilled laborers. Some servants were highly trained craftsman who were expert homebuilders, furniture makers, blacksmiths, weavers, leather smiths, and gardeners. Servants also worked in the fields tending tobacco during the season. Although tending tobacco was the most lucrative, clearing land, building roads, building homes, and growing food was far more important. The tenure of service was five to seven years regardless of race.

The first Virginia colonists did not rely on race at all for identity. The terms "White" or "Negro" were not used to convey identity. The people of the colony were nobility, gentry, artisans, or servants. They identified themselves according to their family, religion, nationality, or social class.

When the first Africans landed at Jamestown, Virginia, in 1619, the men in the colony outnumbered women nine to one. The shortage of women was problematic especially for the indentured class. Of the first twenty Africans to arrive, some were women. Because of the shortage, the colonists welcomed them with open arms. They were pleasantly surprised when they learned that these newcomers were Christians who had been baptized, spoke English, and were somewhat familiar with British customs and laws.

Since race was not an issue among members of the British working class, African women were found suitable for marriage. Marriages between the British working class and Africans took place as early as 1620. Miscegenation spread through the British colonies like wildfire until laws were passed in 1667 to stop it. At the end of the Golden Age in 1640, seventy-two percent of the African population in the colonies had British ancestry.

One of the few histories of an African in America during the Golden Age can be found in early court records. "Antonio the Negro," as he was named, appeared in the 1625 Virginia census. Although identified as a Negro in the census, there was no separate category in the census for race. Antonia was brought into the Virginia colony in 1621. In 1625, British and Colonial law did not permit racial slavery, and in the census Antonio was identified as a servant, not a slave. The term Negro often appeared in legal documents but there was no law stating that Africans had to identify themselves as Negroes. Antonio changed his name to Anthony Johnson. After serving his tenure of indentured servitude, Johnson, as was customary, acquired land and employed his own indentured servants.

In 1640 Anthony Johnson purchased his first property. He had previously married an African servant named Mary and they had four children together. Johnson was a very prosperous man; he owned land, cattle, and his own indentured servants. In the county where he resided there were at least twenty other African men and women who were also free. Thirteen of them owned their own property. From the servants' point of view, indentured servitude appeared to be working according to design.

In that same year, three servants fled a Virginia plantation and were caught and returned to their owner. Two had their servitude extended by four years. However, the third, a black man named John Punch, was sentenced to "serve his said master or his assigns for the time of his natural life." John Punch became the first slave in the British colonies. His enslavement marked the end of the Golden Age.

In 1641 Massachusetts became the first colony to legally recognize slavery. Other states such as Virginia soon followed suit. In 1662 a Virginia law declared that all children born in the colony to a slave mother would be enslaved. Slavery was not only a lifelong condition; it had now become hereditary and could be passed on like skin color from one generation to the next.

The British by tradition believed that they had a right to enslave a non-Christian or a captive taken in a just war. Depending on the circumstances, both definitions fit an African or Indian. But what if the slave converted to Christianity, and learned the nuances of British culture? Should he be freed from bondage and given "freedom dues?" Not according to law. The terms of bondage were determined exclusively by race. Race alone was justification for enslavement, and men who were born free could be enslaved without recourse because of their race. Slavery changed the dynamics of race. People who had lived and worked together were suddenly torn apart.

The members of the British working class, who did not look favorably upon racial slavery, spoke out against it. They, like their African counterpart, had done very well in the indentured servant system and saw no reason to change the system. With all the attention being given to race, in their minds it was much ado about nothing. They worked with African men and married African women and now attempts were being made to separate the races. Wealthy landowners refused to listen to the working class; in their minds the indentured servant system had become obsolete. After their tenure of service, servants moved on and had to be replaced by other servants. There was also the issue of "freedom dues." Servants also started their own businesses after being freed and became fierce competitors. Slavery would eliminate all of the problems that the indentured servant system presented for the white landowners. Slaves would comprise a permanent labor force isolated by race. Seeing the advantages, wealthy landowners signaled the end of the indentured servant system by placing restrictions on available land. Newly freed indentured servants viewed this action in 1676 with contempt. In retaliation, Jamestown was burned to the ground. This disturbance was viewed by the landowners as confirmation that the indentured servant system had run its course and it was time to scrap it, which they did.

Eleven years earlier in 1665, Anthony Johnson had moved his family to Maryland where he had leased a

300-acre plantation before dying five years later. But back in Virginia in 1676, a jury decided the land Johnson left behind could be seized by the government because he was a "Negro and by consequence an alien." In 1705 Virginia declared:

> **All servants imported and brought into this County who were not Christians in their Native Country... shall be slaves. A Negro, mulatto and Indian slaves... shall be held to be real estate.**

> **If any slave resist his master... correcting such slave, and shall happen to be killed in such correction... the master shall be free of all punishment... as if such accident never happened.**

With the enactment of this law, the English colonies introduced a new form of slavery to the world. This new system would prove to be the most sinister form of slavery ever conceived by man. People who had previously identified themselves as Christians, British, Irish, and Dutch suddenly became white male and female.

The White Race becomes a Legal Entity

What the British failed to do at home was accomplished in America. In America, the demographics were such that race could replace the family as the dominant source of identity. Those born in America had no association with the royal family and little if any association with the family back home in Britain. Their ancestors had no impact on the way they lived their lives. Instead of living for the family they choose to live for the race. This presented a unique opportunity for those who would become racial ideologues.

Using a new mandate that authorized racial slavery, the superiority of the white race was legislated into existence. Slavery served as an effective tool to establish and maintain racial dominance. With the power derived from domination, the culture of racial privilege was erected. This culture became a hotbed for breeding racists. Found among the elite class, these racists were the first to abandon ethnic identity to become white male and female. Having secured a position of racial dominance, they made race the cultural focal point.

After asserting racial superiority in the presence of those deemed inferior by law, America's culture of racial privilege was firmly implanted. According to the precedent set, nothing determined one's fitness as an American citizen more so than race. To underline the importance of race, laws that imposed social, political, and economic deprivation were passed and strictly enforced.

Being deprived and rewarded according to one's race was an effective way to attract immigrants. America was the only place on earth where upon entry you were rewarded for being white. But if you were black you were targeted for oppression. Hardships that might normally be viewed as individual or family issues would now be viewed as racial issues because of laws designed to impact the whole race. Seemingly for those relegated to the bottom position, the only way to ward off these hardships was to unify as a race. For those who had never known race as identity, unifying as a race posed a major challenge. This was true for those at the bottom and those on top.

To maintain the top position, steps were taken to consolidate the white base. No immigrant came to America identifying him or herself as a white male or female. The disenfranchised Europeans who composed the majority of the laboring class identified with their ethnicity.[7] The fear among the elite class who were a tiny minority was that the ethnic European would side with Native people and those of African descent to overthrow them.

To increase their numbers, the elite class in Virginia passed a law in 1639 that identified all Europeans as white. The law awarded the privilege of buying land and owning guns to whites only.[8] This law was the first to detail the benefits of living for the white race. Having been the subject of a law, the white race became a legal entity. The term white was used in this instance to encourage Europeans to abandon ethnic identity and separate themselves racially from the Negro and Native American. The law created a third tier in society.

The same societal structure found in Britain was found all over Europe. There were basically two classes, upper and lower. A person's position in society was determined by his or her family. A member of the family could change his or her status by marrying a member of the upper class, but the family as a whole never changed. Until they arrived in America, families in the lower classes in Europe could not change the family's status. Their position at the bottom was permanent because there was no population that could be placed beneath them. In America this changed, and having white skin was enough to put the entire family at the top of the race ladder.

Inventing the Race Card

This change was made possible by the formation of the white and black races. Until it occurred in America, no attempt had been made to unify the white or black race. No people in Europe gave up their ethnic identity to become white in order to dominate the black race. Neither did any people in Africa give up their tribal identity to become black in order to dominate the white race.

The American people were the first to give up their ethnic identity to form a race to dominate another race. This was a boon for members of the European lower classes. For the first time, people who had always been at the bottom found someone beneath them. The people beneath them were Negroes and Native Americans. To give them a sense of superiority, they were pandered to and encouraged to abuse those who were beneath them. People who had a history of looking up to others now found someone to look down on.

Another ploy used by the white elite to expand their numbers was the indoctrination of children. The children of immigrants were taught in kindergarten how to be white. To impose white identity, advocates used one of the most blatantly divisive statements ever uttered by man: "You are members of the superior race." No child can hear this statement from a parent or teacher and not in some way be affected. If you tell a five-year-old child that nothing matters more than your race and that your race is superior, acceptance of the statement is almost guaranteed.

Desperate measures were necessary because these were desperate times. Cultural ties with Britain had been severed. Stripped of their British heritage after the Revolutionary War, the Founding Fathers were hard pressed to find a new identity. They could no longer rely on the British crown, culture, or their British family for identity. They could not go back; they could only go forward. Going forward, they chose race as their identity. To go forward as a white male and female meant that they were a people without a history. No people before them lived solely for the pleasure of the white race.

To acquire a history, they laid claim to everything produced by people with white skin. Before they appeared as the self-appointed agents of the white race, no one had ever claimed to represent all white people. The Greeks, the Romans, not even the British had the audacity to make such an outrageous claim. They only claimed to represent those who shared their families and their culture. There was never an inference made to suggest that all whites were Greek, Roman, or British.

America's only King?

With no cultural history to fall back on, America's Founding Fathers chose race as the repository of power. The position that had traditionally been held by a family was awarded to the race. Throughout history, family had played an important role in governing nations. According to British tradition, greatness was bestowed upon a person by his family not his race; to some extent, this was illustrated in the life of George Washington.

Washington became a great man due to the influence of his family. His identity was formed by his family, not his race. It was his half brother, Lawrence, who instilled in him a sense of nobility and the desire to become a leader. Lawrence passed away in 1752 and George ultimately inherited the Mount Vernon estate. Groomed since childhood to become America's first king, Washington was ready when the opportunity presented itself. His lifelong ambition became a reality after the Revolutionary War when his men, according to legend, chose him as America's king. His reign only lasted thirteen days, but according to British standards he was not really qualified to be a king.

Kingship is given life by family, not government. It is a position held within the institution of family and is passed down through the family. In a monarchy, the power of governance belongs to the family, not to the government. This keeps the focus of society fixed on family. The king is the official head of the royal family. The kingship of George Washington according to these criteria was an aberration. He could not assemble a royal family as his family ties had been severed by the war. Family in Britain, being loyal to the crown, severed ties with their American cousins after the Revolutionary War.

The role of the royal family in a monarchy is almost as important as that of the king's. The king's power is shared with his family. It's the duty of the royal family to use its' power to promote the general welfare of the nation by supporting development in areas such as education, art, music, science, sports, industry, medicine, and spirituality.

A vibrant royal family that is dedicated to developing the full potential of its citizenry is considered a monarchy's greatest cultural asset.

George Washington had no such family and neither did any of America's Founding Fathers. No one was qualified to become king. None of the Founding Fathers had the esteemed family heritage required to establish the traditions of a monarch. The traditional standard bearers of the culture are the members of the royal family. The royal family is not only the cultural leader of the nation but also exemplifies the family ideal. They keep family at the forefront of the nation's consciousness. American governance made no provision for the establishment of a royal family. There was no American family qualified to act as the standard barriers of the culture. This created a tremendous vacuum.

America's answer to the royal family was the first family. The first family served only as a façade. It was given no authority to act on behalf of the government. The first lady to some limited degree had the power to dictate social policy but she could only do so as a private citizen not as an official of the state. No one else in the first family had any authority to speak or act on behalf of the government.

The American system of government greatly reduced the power and influence of family on the society. Instead of seeding the power of governance to a family it was seeded to the race. For the Founders, empowering the race was the most effective way to share power. Having chosen the racial path, preserving white identity became the topmost priority and to accomplish this feat the focus of identity was shifted to externals.

Prior to America's founding, every major civilization yielded to internal influences and tribal and ethnic identity flourished. God, family, tribe, and nationality were major contributors to the collective identity. People lived internal lives; there were no external civilizations. Although America became the first nation of race, it did not begin that way.

End Notes
Chapter One

[1] Robert S. Schwartz, M.D., "Race Is a Poor Measure," New England Journal of Medicine, Vol. 344, No. 18 (2001).

[2] Frank M. Snowden,Jr., Before Color Prejudice: The Ancient View of Blacks (Cambridge: Harvard University Press, 1983) 16–17.

[3] Plato, The Last Days of Socrates, (New York: Penguin, 1995) 97–110.

[4] Alastair Bonnett, "Construction of Whiteness in European and American Anti-Racism," Race, Identity and Citizenship: A Reader, ed. Rodolfo D. Torres, Louis F. Mirón, Jonathan Xavier Inda (San Francisco: Blackwell Publishing, 1999) 200–218.

[5] WGBH/PBS, Africans in America: America's Journey Through Slavery (1998).

[6] Theodore W. Allen, The Invention of the White Race (New York: Verso, 1994).

[7] "Landholding by African-Americans in the seventeenth century was significant, both for the extent of it, and because much of it, possibly the greater portion, was secured by headright. This particular fact establishes perhaps more forcefully than any other circumstance the normal social status accorded to African-Americans, a status that was practically as well as theoretically incompatible with a system of racial oppression."

[8] Most significant are the Virginia court records of legal recognition of normal social standing and mobility for African-Americans.

Illustrative cases are found frequently in the Northampton and Accomack county records:

- In 1624, The Virginia Colony Court adjudicated an admiralty-type case, in which the Court considered the testimony of John Phillip, a mariner, identified as "a negro Christened in England…"
- A Negro named Brase came to Jamestown in 1625. He was assigned to Governor Francis Wyatt as a "servant". Although there is no record of the terms of this assignment, there is no suggestion that, "being a Negro," he was to be a lifetime bond-laborer.
- African-Americans who were not bond-laborers made contracts for work or for credit, engaged in commercial as well as land transactions, with European-Americans, and in the related court proceedings they stood on the same footing as European-Americans.
- Emannuel Rodriggus arrived in Virginia before 1647. He became a dealer in livestock on the Eastern Shore. As early as 1652/63 there was recorded a bill of sale signed with his mark, assigning to merchant John Cornelys "one Cowe collered Blacke, aged about fowre years…being my owne breed." Thereafter, Rodriggus and other African-Americans frequently appear as buyers and sellers and sometimes as donors, of livestock in court records that reflect the assumption of the right of African-Americans to accumulate and dispose of property, an assumption of legal parity of buyer and seller.
- The Indian king Debeada of the Mussaugs gave to Jone, daughter of Anthony Johnson, 100 acres of land on the South side of Pungoteague Creek…In 1657 Emmanuell Cambow, a "Negro" was granted ownership of fifty acres of land in James City County…In 1669, Robert Jones (or Johns), a York County tailor… bargained & sold unto John Harris Negro all the estate rite (right) title & Inheritance…in fiftie Acres of Land…in New Kent County."
- A series of land transactions—lease, sub-lease, and re-lese—were conducted by Emanuell Rodriggus with three separate individuals over a ten-year period, 1662–1672.
- The following are well documented cases of seventeenth century African-American land owners:
- Land patent granted to Anthony Johnson, on 250 acres for transport of 5 persons: Tho Benrose, Peter Bughby, Antho: Cripps, John Gessorol[?], Richard Johnson. (Virginia Land Patent Book No. 2, p. 326. 24 July 1651.) 108.

- Patent granted to John Johnson, son of Anthony Johnson, on 550 acres, on Great Nassawattocks Creek, adjacent to land granted to Anthony Johnson, for the transportation of eleven persons: John Edwards, Wm Routh, Thos. Yowell, Fran. Maland, Wm Price, John Owe, Dorothy Reely, Rich Hamstead, Law[rence] Barnes. (Virginia Land Patent Book, No. 3, p. 101. 10 May 1652.)
- Patent on 100 acres bounded by lands owned by Anthony, Richard's father, and by brother John Johnson, granted by Governor Richard Bennett to Richard Johnson, "Negro," for the transportation of two bond-laborers: William Ames and William Vincent. (Virginia Land Patent Book, No. 3, p. 294. 21 November 1654.)
- There was no suggestion that African-Americans were barred from the privilege of importing bond-laborers prior to 1670. The enactment of such a ban in 1670 clearly implied that it was an accepted practice prior to that time.

[9] Winthrop D. Jordan, White Over Black: American Attitudes Towards the Negro 1550-1812 (Chapel Hill: University of North Carolina Press, 1968) 86–98.

[10] William Waller Hening, ed., "Virginia Slavery Act X" (1639-40) The Statutes at Large; Being a Collection of all the Laws of Virginia, From the First Session of the Legislature in the year 1619.vols.1 and II (New York:R & W & G Bartow, 1823) 226.

2

Constructing White Identity

It would be hard to imagine someone writing a book about what it means to be white. Most white people don't consider themselves to be part of a race that needs examining. They are the natural order of things.
—James Saynor, 1995

The Whitewashing of America

The first generations born to British immigrants in America had great difficulty preserving British

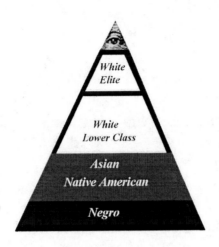

identity. Their sense of being British was imperiled by a lack of exposure to British culture. These children were taught to speak the English language but did not identify with the culture that produced it. They were born in the wilderness far away from the sights, sounds, tastes, smells, and feel of British society. They never saw the Thames River, the British Museum, Westminster Abbey, Cambridge, Oxford, St. Andrews Cathedral, Edinburgh Castle, and numerous other sights.

As children few were taught to live like their brethren in Britain. Their cultural experience was limited to the colonies, which in the early 1700s had few cultural landmarks. There were no palaces, no towering Cathedrals, no stately avenues, no great institutions of higher learning, and, above all, no history as a nation.

Some of the elite parents of the third generation born in the colonies made no effort to transfer British identity. The effort was not made because they did not know themselves as British. Even though they were subjects of the crown, their identity was not tied to the crown or the family back in Britain. After residing in the colonies for generations, few attempts were made to contact the family or return to the British mainland.

Few children born in the colonies were given the opportunity to visit the homeland of their ancestors. The Jefferson family is a case in point. Thomas Jefferson, the elder, was born in Gynnedd, Wales in 1653; his father was Samuel Jefferson. He came to America in the 1670s and settled on a plantation in Henrico County, Virginia named "Snowden".[1] When he arrived in Virginia he did not identify himself as a white male. The first Virginia colonists did not rely on race for identity. The terms "white" or "Negro" were not used to convey identity. The people of the colony were nobility, gentry, artisans, or servants, and they identified themselves according to their family, religion, nationality, or social class.

Jefferson married Mary Branch in 1677 and they had three children, Thomas, Martha, and Mary, who were the first generation of Jeffersons born in America. Although Thomas Jefferson was proud of his heritage and named his plantation after his childhood home, he never returned to Wales. Neither did his son, Thomas Jefferson, who was born in 1677. Jefferson married Mary Field in 1697 and fathered seven children, Field, Judith, Alice, Thomas, Peter, Mary, and Martha. Peter, his son born in 1707, married Jane Randolph in 1738 and fathered Jane, Mary, Elizabeth, Peter Field, Lucy, Anna, Randolph, Thomas, and another son whose name is unknown. There is no history of any of the Jefferson family returning to Wales.

Thomas Jefferson had no cultural heritage that he could claim as his own. He did not claim British heritage because the family's cultural ties with Britain had been severed. Although not identified as British, the key fundamentals of British culture such as the language, religion, and class that were taught to him were not identified as British. Jefferson spoke English, was a Christian, and was a member of the noble class, but the identity he assumed was distinctly non-British.

Jefferson was one of a few male members of the noble class born in colonial America that identified as white males. These men had several things in common as their fathers had severed cultural ties with Britain and they were of the second or third generation born in the colony and their fathers owned slaves.[2]

At the time no serious attempt had been made to consolidate the white race. Having had their cultural ties severed with their ancestors, the sons of British nobles who became the Founding Fathers were hard pressed to find an identity. For the first time in history, race was given precedent over culture.

The American white males were the first people to totally sell out to race, a race that had not yet been consolidated. When Jefferson claimed to be a white male, the white race as an entity unto itself had not been formed. At this juncture, being white meant being a part of something that existed in concept only. It only existed as a concept because the vast majority of people had not chosen race as their identity.

The white male could only be found among the elite. The noble class comprised only about eighteen percent of the population. The majority population in the colony at the time was of common stock. Descendants of the commoner had no problem with cultural identity even though it separated people according to class.

One's birth determined one's class status and the mixing of the classes was not allowed. A commoner was not allowed to even dress as a nobleman. Although the color issue was raised in Britain, it had no power to bridge the gap that existed between the classes. The dynamics of British culture would not allow it. A person's status in society was not determined by his color; it was determined by his class.

The same class distinctions that were found in Britain were also observed in the colony. The noble class and the working class did not freely associate with each other; class structure kept people separated. Nobles did not marry among the lower classes and neither did the lower classes marry nobles. When it first manifested, white male identity was exclusive; it was not shared with the lower classes. Being a white male was about maintaining the elite status of the nobleman. To do so, class distinctions had to be maintained, which made the consolidation of the white race impossible. The common man was not allowed to sit at the table of the nobleman. It was not until after the Revolutionary War that a serious effort was made to consolidate the white race. The leader of the movement was Thomas Jefferson who became the third president of the United States.

Upper and Lower Class Whites Unite

After the Revolutionary War, the separation between the upper and lower class had not changed. Freedom had no impact on the class structure of society. White identity was not clearly defined. The white race was divided by class. To consolidate the race, the upper class had to draw closer to the lower class. The elimination of class by sharing wealth equally within the race was not an option. What Thomas Jefferson did to raise the status of lower class whites was to create a new lower class. This new lower class consisted of blacks and Native Americans.

In 1790, when the census was introduced, there were approximately 800,000 blacks in America. This population combined with Native Americans was identified as the new lower class. To raise the social status of whites that had previously comprised the lower class, privileges were extended to them that were denied to blacks and Native Americans. Among these privileges were citizenship, ownership of land, and the rights to vote, hold public office, and bear arms.

Before Jefferson stepped into the limelight, the superiority of the white race had not been officially declared. The words, "You are members of the superior race" had not been uttered to the members of the lower class who outnumbered the elite ten to one.

The passage of laws that granted and denied privileges based on race allowed the white elite to share the power of racial domination with lower class whites. The elite class was a tiny minority, and fearing the loss of their power they drove a wedge between the white lower class and blacks. Laws were passed to prohibit interracial marriages. Any child born of an African mother could now be enslaved. By drafting laws that divided the races the world's first culture of racial privilege was legislated into existence.[3]

Thomas Jefferson, using the census, laid the foundation for the formation of the white race. After laying the foundation, which amounted to allocating space, the construction of white identity was taken up in earnest. Theodore Allen in his book, *The Invention of the White Race*,[4] offers this vivid description of the process:

> *The knowledge, ideologies, norms, and practices of whiteness and the accompanying "white race" were invented in the U.S. as part of a system of racial oppression designed to solve a particular problem in colonial Virginia.*

The knowledge, ideologies, norms, and practices of whiteness affect how we think about race, what we see when we look at certain physical features, how we build our own racial identity, how we operate in the world, and what we "know" about our place in it. Whiteness is shaped and maintained by a full array of social institutions— legal, economic, political, educational, religious, and cultural. Individuals and groups affected by whiteness in turn influence and shape these institutions. In response to social forces whiteness is constantly evolving, and as a result the constellations of people who are seen as white have changed over time.

Whiteness serves to preserve the position of a ruling white elite who benefit economically from the labor of other white people and people of color. Whiteness, as knowledge, ideology, norms, and practices, determines who qualifies as "white" and maintains a race and class hierarchy in which people who qualify as white disproportionately control power and resources. Within the group of white people, a small minority of elites hold the reins of the group's power and resources. From this powerful position they dictate the course of society.

After being cajoled by the white elite to secure their position of power, the white lower class has never strayed from the fold, not even during the Civil War when their whiteness was put to the ultimate test. To prove how much they valued whiteness, men who did not own slaves gave up their lives to protect the rights of those who did. For taking up arms, the ultimate privilege was bestowed upon them: the privilege of dying for the race. There was only one thing greater than living for the race and that was dying for it; and those who died were extended the honor of being buried by slaves.For the ruling elite and the working class, whiteness had value as property. In her massive *Harvard Law Review* article, "Whiteness as Property," Cheryl Harris argues that whiteness has been so tied to the right to own property as to itself come to constitute a legally recognizable, usable, and cherished form of property, *possessed by all whites*. The attempted reduction of Blacks, but not whites, to "objects of property" in slavery and the expropriation of Indian land via legal processes that "established whiteness as perquisite to the exercise of enforceable property rights," created, in Harris's view, an enduring set of expectations that whiteness had a value as property.[5]

Harris specifically notes that the concept of whiteness as property persists in legal definitions of racial identity in that those categorized as white enjoy the "right to use and enjoy" their racial position. Whiteness is simultaneously an aspect of identity and a property interest; it is something that can both be experienced and deployed as a resource. It has utility in both the pursuit of happiness and the pursuit of property and forms part of the connective tissue between the two.[6]

End Notes
Chapter Two

[1] Conor C. O'Brien, Thomas Jefferson: Radical and Racist, <u>The Atlantic Monthly</u>, Vol. 278, No. 4 (October 1996) 53–74.

[2] Winthrop D. Jordan, <u>White Over Black</u> :<u>American Attitudes Toward the Negro 1550 – 1812</u> (University of North Carolina Press, 1968) 430–434.

[3] Theodore W. Allen, <u>The Invention of the White Race</u> (Verso: 1991).

[4] Allen.

[5] Cheryl Harris, "Whiteness as Property," <u>Harvard Law Review</u> [online] 1993 http://scholar.google.com 1721, 1724.

[6] Harris, 1734.

3

Tying Culture to Race

Blurring the Color Line

Even though the British were the first people to sow the
seeds of color bigotry, they never considered trading
in their cultural identity for race. Try as they may, the
British could not separate themselves from their ethnicity.
After all, it was the culture, not color, that made Britain
great.

Although color was made an issue, the sense of
being British was deeper than color. It existed long before
color was introduced. The British had white skin but they
always saw themselves as distinctly different from other
people who had white skin. This was even true in their
own culture. Even though the commoner had white skin,

was drawn in the sand and everything on one side of the line was white and everything on the other side of the line was black or "other."

Anything produced by Africans such as art, music, dance, literature, science, technology, religion, sports, diet, language, and architecture, regardless of its cultural or ethnic background, was considered black, and anything produced by Europeans was considered white. Lumping the cultural jewels produced by different cultures together within a particular race was the system America used to amalgamate the races. Hundreds of different cultures exist among members of the same race and more than one race has been known to share the same culture. Culture and race are not synonymous but in America the two were merged in order to connect everyone within the race. Americans value who they are racially more than who they are culturally. American culture is about living for the race. The external connection created by race is valued more than the diversity created by culture.

White identity is an external connection; to preserve it an external civilization was erected.[4] The vehicle used to construct this civilization was race. Race, one's external identity, determines your position in American society. Race by design has two stations, one on top and one at the bottom. The top position was reserved for whites while the bottom position was reserved for blacks.

The power of projection was used to secure and maintain the top position. Projecting an image and attaching it to the race is how the process of racialism worked. These projections took place on the physical and mental plane. On the physical plane a positive image was projected by attaching wealth, culture, family, and religion to the white race. By identifying everything it owned and controlled as a racial asset, the superior race provided physical evidence of its dominant status.[5]

On the mental plane a negative image of the inferior race was projected. Inspired by economic aspirations, this distorted image served as a catalyst for engaging in the grossest forms of inhumanity. The mere sight of dark skin was enough in some minds to provoke a response that might be lethal.

In America, showing up black could cost you your life but showing up white won you favor. America's first love was the white race. "Without the white race America would be nothing." "Everything great about America is due to the white race." These are the sentiments that built the nation. Central among them has been the quest to preserve white identity. In America, success is an external image. The people in the best position to pursue this image are those with white skin.[6]

Human beings, however, have a dual composition, an outer and inner being. To fully access the human experience, the outer as well as the inner being must be engaged. Living for the race, the inner being becomes inoperable. The ability to keep the inner being bound up has been the key to American prosperity. People who are focused only on externals cannot pursue internal life. They fall prey to materialism. Materialism, as America has shown, is the best tool one can use to preserve racial identity. In America, the decorations on the tree of life are valued more than the tree. Of all the decorations on the tree, the one that America values most is race. No one can live outside of race in America; the system will not allow it. It was created to preserve white identity.

Top and Bottom

To establish the top position someone has to occupy the bottom. With no one beneath you the claim of supremacy cannot be supported. The two positions, top and bottom, exist in space. We cannot see, feel, hear, or taste space. Some of the most powerful social and political institutions are premised on the notion that space is a thing. For example, a state—by definition, a territorially based entity—cannot exist independently of space. States are fixed in space, set off by non-overlapping geographical boundaries that distinguish them from other states. People jealously guard their personal space as though it were a valuable possession. They hope strangers will stay out of "their" space. When people want to be alone, they tell others that they need "their" space.

Space is expressed in terms of its dimensions, proportions, area, volume, and location. In order for space to exist on top, there must be space at the bottom. The driving force behind the quest for white identity has always been to occupy the top space. No one can occupy this space without engaging in some form of oppression.[7]

Anyone who claims the top position must assume the role of the oppressor. Those who live for the pleasure of the white race have a history of oppression. To perform as the oppressor they must engage in some form of mental or physical suppression. Native Americans were the first to be targeted. In this instance, the catalyst for aggression was greed, a principle characteristic that drives white identity.

Greed can provide justification for all forms of oppression. Oppression produces the best results when the people being targeted live external lives. In this regard,

Native Americans presented a major challenge because they lived their lives internally. Who they were internally was valued more than who they were externally. Their external presence was only a shadow of the inner self, which ultimately made them targets for extermination.

Internally there is no top or bottom; everyone is equal. Everyone is guided by custom and tradition. To claim the bottom position, Native Americans would have to view themselves externally. That would mean giving up internal life. That was unacceptable. The psychology used by whites to impose external life on Native Americans failed. As a last resort, murder and exile was used to subdue them. Although forcibly positioned at the bottom, the Native American did not claim the bottom position. They continued to resist by refusing to live external lives.

The second people targeted for the bottom position were Africans. To impose bondage on the African, a restraining device in the form of Negro identity was used. Negro identity, like white identity, is an external perception, the difference being that Negro identity positioned the African at the bottom.[8]

Like their Native American counterparts, members of the Fon, Yoruba, Ibo, Fanti, Ashanti, Mandingo, and Jolof tribes refused to be bound by externals. They also lived internal lives. They were guided from within by customs and traditions handed down by their ancestors. Chided, they refused to cede the power to be identified to anyone other than their ancestors. Who they were internally had nothing to do with color. Honoring the customs and traditions of their ancestors kept their internal identity alive. Giving up internal life to become a Negro was to enter into the ranks of the walking dead.

Historically, state legislatures attempted to coerce individuals of mixed black-white race lineage to identify with blackness through a two-part framework, with both parts being rooted in the language of the law. First, many state legislatures promulgated legal definitions that afforded mixed black-white race individuals a separate identity from Negroes but placed them "squarely in the same category as Blacks with all the legal disadvantages that accompanied" such status.[11] Secondly, the majority of state legislatures then effectively did away with stand-alone mixed black-white identity in favor of legally espousing the rule of hypodescent. Hypodescent is the institutional practice of assigning racially mixed people to the status of the subordinate group. Pursuant to this approach, even individuals of primarily white skin color were effectively coerced into black racial identification by law.[12] Because they were of mixed heritage, they were rejected by both Anglos and Africans alike. Access to their ancestral languages, religions, family, tribe, nation, and people was cut off.

Even though the mother was present, African identity was not transferred to these children. The institutions were not available to support the transfer. There was no village, nation, family, tribe, culture, or people from which to draw identity. The mothers were not even allowed to speak their native language. These children had nothing internal to embrace and could only live external lives. There was no father for them and the relationship with their mothers was non-traditional. Even though the mothers may have held on to their cultural identity and not identified themselves racially, they viewed their children differently because they were of mixed blood. When they saw their children, they did not see Africans; they saw what society saw—a

Negro, and that was who their children became. Using the Negro child he fathered, the white male tried to break the back of the African resistance.

In the mid-1740s mulattoes began to appear amongst the enslaved population. They had the first experience of living for the black race. Fredrick Douglas, a prominent mulatto of African descent, cloaked himself in Negro identity. From birth, he saw life through Negro eyes. Living for the race was the only life he knew. He could not identify with African culture as his African connection was cut off. No African people claimed him. He was of mixed heritage, born of an African mother who only saw him four or five times in her life. She died when he was seven and his British father was never identified. It was suggested, although never proven, that his mother had been raped by a man she did not know.

Slaves were often blindfolded before they were raped to protect the identity of the rapist. It was obvious that these rapists were not African because the children they fathered had fair skin, blue eyes, and curly hair. In most instances, the father was the master or the overseer but seldom, if ever, did anyone come forward to take credit for his handiwork.

What started some hundred years earlier with the Native American and the African, finally became a reality when the first Negroes identified themselves. It's quite ironic, however, that the first Negroes were fathered by white males. These white males were not there as fathers for their children. The children had no father in their lives. No one claimed them as family. The Negro was born outside the family of mankind. It was from a position at the bottom that Negroes were forced to live their lives.

Attempts made to increase their numbers by bringing Africans into the fold were soundly rejected. Negro identifies race. Race is external identity that has no internal dimensions. Living external life, the only connection a person makes with others is external. Africans at the time had no external connections; they were connected internally. External attempts by the Negro to bridge the gap between them using race were unproductive.

Even though it was indeed the turning point, the appearance of the first Negro did not have the immediate impact on the African population that whites desired. Other than a few mothers and their children, there were no mass conversions to Negro identity by Africans. The internal connection between the African people remained intact. In 1740 there was an estimated 400,000 slaves in America; less than three percent of this population had been born in America. Even if the entire three percent identified themselves as Negroes, it was not enough to provide a stable base upon which to build white identity. After one hundred years of African resistance showed no signs of wilting, a new threat was looming on the horizon: the "English only" rule.

Linguistic Subjugation

To be familiar with all the nuances of the culture, a person had to speak English. To establish a culture of race, a language of race was critical.[13] With the subjugation and suppression of Africans, came a language that labeled them 'chattels', 'property', and beasts. This sort of oppressive language appeared in legal documents, political speech, and religious discourse.[14] Dehumanization is most likely when the target group can be readily identified as a separate category of people belonging to a distinct racial or ethnic group that the perpetrators regard as inferior.[15] A common form of disparagement is the use of language to redefine the victims so they will be seen as warranting the aggression. The distance between the linguistic dehumanization of a people and their actual suppression is not great.[16] When victims cannot present a worthy self, it becomes exceedingly difficult to exert a direct and powerful demand for moral and humane treatment. This language was extracted from the body of English.[17] So that they might participate in the culture, Africans were prodded to speak English. To fix the African tongue, the "English only" rule was enforced.

Only one language could be spoken aloud: English. Any slave who spoke his tribal language aloud ran the risk of having his tongue cut out. To communicate in their native tongue, slaves were forced to whisper. Because of the "English only" rule the first generation of children born into slavery did not speak the language of their ancestors; they spoke English. The English they were taught was adulterated by design. An educated slave was viewed as a threat to society and to eliminate the threat laws were passed that made it illegal to educate slaves.

To impede their learning capabilities, slaves were not taught standard English. Selected words and phrases were doctored in a way that only the slave and the owner knew their precise meaning. This made educating slaves very difficult for anyone coming from the outside that did not know the idiom. The introduction of English to the slave was a one-dimensional affair that consisted only of the spoken word. The other two dimensions, reading and writing, were withheld to prevent slaves from documenting the atrocities that were being committed against them. Furthermore, the spoken word was bastardized before being taught in order to adulterate the Negro tongue. Through a concocted system of linguistic devolution, the Negro was stamped with an indelible mark that is still audible today. Silencing the African tongue proved to be invaluable to the process of infusing Negro identity because it severed the cultural connection with Africa. Language is the foundation of culture. When the African tongue was silenced, African culture in America collapsed.

The English language was the perfect medium for infusing Negro identity. Owing to the perverse nature of English, precepts could be articulated that could not be conveyed using any tribal tongue. There were no corresponding words to express them. Profanity is a case in point. English is the world's most perverse language. There is more profanity in English than there is in any other language. Most African languages have no profanity. Profanity conjures up negative stereotypes. Introducing profanity proved to be an effective way to degrade the Negroes consciousness.

Teaching English to the African was different from teaching English to the Negro. The African spoke the language of their ancestors. There were English words and concepts that had no African derivative and African words and concepts that had no English derivative. In African society, there was no culture of race. Nothing people produced in terms of art, music, dance, literature, science, technology, religion, sports, diet, language, and architecture was identified racially. The concept of race was completely foreign. There were no people in African society who claimed to represent the race. To be accepted, the concept of race had to be communicated in terms that Africans could understand. The language people speak shapes their perception and understanding of who they are. To change that perception everyone involved has to speak the same language. Because the Africans had already formed an identity, this made teaching English very difficult. This was not the case however with the Negro.

The Negro was born in America and had no culture of his own. There was no Negro language or religion. The Negro was an empty vessel. Using the language of race, the Negro psyche was shaped to facilitate the desires of the owner. One of the first things taught using the language was to identify oneself as a Negro. "I am a Negro." Speaking these words and understanding them was one of the first steps used to form Negro identity. In some instances the term "nigger" was used. Concepts were introduced that were not African in origin and race was one of them.

To address each other, the Negro was taught to use unflattering terms that were demeaning and disrespectful. Of course they did not know this at the time. Racially charged English was used to tie the perceptual reality of the Negro to negative space. Using language, space was created for the Negro to occupy. The term Negro not only referred to the body, it also referred to the space that the Negro occupied.

There were unflattering terms used to identify Negro space. The Negro did not live in a house; the Negro lived in a shack. Everything found in Negro space was tainted by the terms that they were taught to define them.

There were very few terms used to identify Negro space, which served to limit their perception. These terms were all negative, but the Negro was not told that they were negative. A case in point is the term "nigger." Negroes who used the term were not told that it was negative. This misuse of language was found very amusing.

Conditioned by language that created negative space, the only identity the Negro could project was race. The limited use of the language would not allow Negroes to project any other identity. This occurred before the concept of race was clearly understood. The language was packaged and delivered in such a way that just speaking it tied the Negro to the race. Polluted sound was used to infuse Negro identity.

Since being introduced to English, negativity has been a staple of the Negro mindset. The Negro was taught to speak and view himself in a negative light. Everything Negro was thought to be negative but the Negro did not understand the language of negativity. Being ignorant, Negroes did not know the true meaning of the terms they used. Nothing has a greater impact on how you are perceived by others than your mastery of the language. Those who use a language without having a true understanding of word meaning will always be perceived to be ignorant even though they may be brilliant. Brilliance is of little value if it cannot be articulated. Conceptualizing without the ability to articulate can be extremely frustrating and this frustration was common among the first Negroes. Not only could they not express what they were feeling and thinking in words, the words they used were vitiated. To confuse the Negro, positive terms were negative and negative terms were positive. Bad was good, and good was bad. In all of this perplexity, the Negro was held captive by a language he did not create or master.

In referring to one another, terms were used that were derogatory and undignified. To compliment another Negro it was not uncommon to use the term "nigger." Using negative terms as positive have a desensitizing affect. Even though they are uttered with no contempt, the negative connotation remains. Negative sounds are rooted in negativity. Used as terms of endearment, does not change their subtle nature. There is no such thing as clean coal. Coal is by nature dirty. Washing coal will not clean it; the same is true for "nigger." "Nigger" identifies filth and nothing can change its nature. The sound is a subtle contaminant that feeds the negative mindset.

Examples of this negative mindset were revealed time and time again in interviews of former slaves. Sarah Debro, age 90, was interviewed on July 24, 1937, in Durham, N.C. by Travis Jordan. These were some of her comments:

> *"I was born in Orange County way back some time in the fifties. Miz Polly White Cain and Marse Dr. Cain was my white folks. Marse Cain's plantation joined Mr. Paul Cameron's land. Marse Cain owned so many niggers that he didn't know his own slaves when he meets them on the road. Sometimes he would stop them and say: 'whose niggers are you?' They'd say, 'We's Marse Cain niggers.' Then he would say, 'I's Marse Cain and drive on."*

Everything that Sarah Debro revealed in her interview was negative but it was presented as if it was positive. The Negro could talk all day and night in the negative and think that it was positive. When a person speaks negatively, he thinks negatively, even though it is represented in a positive context. Negroes were taught by manipulating the language to view life from a negative perspective. White folks were the only ones who spoke and thought in the positive. If a Negro spoke and thought in the positive, he was accused of trying to be white. When life is viewed from a negative perspective, the viewer always looks for and identifies with the negative. Using derogatory terms such as nigger is a prime example.

The term nigger and the concept of nigger originated in the minds of men who were deluded by white skin. Their identity is unknown, but no single act has done more to tie race to culture in America than the invention of this term. The first nigger had white skin. The concept identified a behavior that was prevalent in the white population long before the term was coined. According to the description, niggers are lustful, conniving, unclean, disrespectful, irresponsible, deceitful, and sexually perverted. Even though the earliest examples of a nigger in America were white, the culture did not give the white race credit. It would not award whites even though they fit the description, the ignoble distinction of being identified as a nigger. That title was reserved exclusively for the Negro.

A case in point was James Henry Hammond (November 15, 1807 – November 13, 1864). Hammond was a politician from South Carolina. He served as a United States Representative from 1835 to 1836, Governor of South Carolina from 1842 to 1842, and United States

Senator from 1857 to 1860. He was the brother-in-law of Wade Hampton II and uncle of Wade Hampton III.

A Democrat, Hammond was perhaps best known during his lifetime as an outspoken defender of slavery and states' rights. It was Hammond who coined the phrase, "Cotton is King" in an 1858 speech to the Senate. In 1839, he purchased a young female slave with an infant daughter. He took the woman as his mistress and fathered several of her children before replacing her with her twelve-year-old daughter. His other slaves faired no better. It was reported in 1841 that seventy-eight of his chattel died in a ten-year period.

His Secret and Sacred Diaries reveal that his appetites did not end there. He describes without embarrassment his "familiarities and dalliances" with four teenage nieces. He blamed the seductiveness of the "extremely affectionate" young women. Any Negro who engaged in such deviant sexual behavior would certainly be tagged with the nigger label, but not James Henry Hammond; he was celebrated as a cultural icon, a tribute to his race. Because of his high position and unlimited resources at the time, there was not one Negro in America that could out-nigger James Henry Hammond.[18]

End Notes
Chapter Three

(1) David Roediger, "The Pursuit of Whiteness: Property, Terror and Expansion, 1790-1860" Michael A. Morrison & James Brewer Stewart, ed., Race and the Early Republic (Rowman & Littlefield, 2002) 5–8.

(2) Roediger, 14–18.

(3) Roediger, 19.

(4) William G. Roy, Making Societies (Boston: SAGE Publications, 2001) 96.

(5) Roy, 97.

(6) Roy, 98.

(7) Roy, 49.

(8) Roy, 50.

(9) Richard Middleton IV, "The Historical Legal Construction of Black Racial Identity of Mixed Black-White Individuals: The Role of State Legislatures" [online] 2008), http://papers.ssrn.com

(10) Roy, 2.

(11) Roy, 2.

(12) Roy, 2.

(13) Legrand H. Clegg II, Editor & Publisher, "Ebonics: A Serious Analysis of African American Speech Patterns" MAAT News [online] 1997, www.melanet.com/clegg_series/maat.html

(14) Haig Bosmajian, The Language of Oppression (Lanham: University Press of America, 1983) 1.

(15) James Waller, Becoming Evil: How Ordinary People Commit Genocide and Mass Murder (Oxford: Oxford University Press, 2002), 246.

(16) Waller, 247.

(17) Waller, 248.

(18) James W. Loewen, Lies Across America (New York: Touchstone, 1999) 270–272.

4

Tying the Family to the Race

Infusing Racial Identity

Tying the family to the race was another technique used in America to infuse racial identity. The white family derived the greatest benefit from living for the race. Having been given the opportunity, entire families took advantage. Such was the case of the Calhoun family of South Carolina.[1] Patrick Calhoun, the father of John C. Calhoun, immigrated to this country with his family when he was five years old. The Calhoun family hailed from Donegal Island, Ireland, where they were members of the lower class. The family was of meager means and received little in terms of standing in their homeland. Their arrival in America, however, changed their lot.

Prior to coming to this country, there is no documented evidence of the family having any contact with Africans. Contact with Africans in America seems to have changed the family's plight. Catapulted by slavery, the Calhoun family went on to become one of America's most prominent families of the race. John C. Calhoun, a fiery Southern Statesman and protégé of Thomas Jefferson, rode the wave of racial bigotry all the way to the White House. He earned the iniquitous reputation of being America's most ardent defender of slavery.

Sixty years after slavery became law, a decision was made to produce what we now know as the African American family. Prior to 1720, no serious effort had been made to breed slaves. According to estimates, the slave population in the colonies in 1725 was about 80,000. Only five percent of this population was female. Although slavery became the law of the land in 1660, only two percent of the slave population in 1725 had been born in the colonies. In 1720 it was even less. Ninety-eight percent of the slaves that had been imported were males. Some of the first arrivals did not see an African woman for sixty years. With no women for the men to associate with, the slave family could not be produced. From 1660 to 1720, there are no records of a slave child being born in the colonies.

It was not until the 1740s that a noticeable change in this demographic occurred. The number of female slaves quadrupled during that decade, and by 1750 the ratio of male to female slaves being imported was fifty-fifty.[2] This shift occurred because breeding slaves made more economic sense than importing them. There was always a percentage of the imported slaves that did not survive the middle passage. Many of the survivors got

Slaves on Edisto Island, S.C., 1862

injured and others became very ill. A less costly alternative surfaced in the 1750s: domestic slave production.[3] After ten years of operation, the North American colonies earned the reputation of being the slave breeding grounds of the world. In the 1790s, Virginia, Maryland, and Delaware exported more slaves than they imported.

Domestic Breeding

Some of the first specimens of the African American family were produced in laboratories known as *slave factories.* Conditions in the slave factories were not conducive to raising a family. Men in these facilities were forced to impregnate women.[4] The first generation of slaves that came from these breeding mills was produced under the threat of death. Some of the more courageous women aborted their children, committed suicide, or murdered the child after it was born. Hundreds of women and men gave up their lives in defiance. To force them into submission, they were tortured. The torture included castration.

The purpose of the slave factory was not to produce families; it was to produce labor.[5] Allowing a family to form was considered a liability. Men and women were separated in the factory. The only time men and women were allowed to associate was during intercourse.

The identity of the father was kept from the child. To keep the male's identity secret, the women were blindfolded. To further ensure that no family formed, just before the mother and child were sold the children were swapped. The woman was sold with someone else's child. She was then taken away to an unfamiliar place where no visible signs of her culture existed. No one used her tribal name, no one spoke her tribal language, and any attempt she made to honor tribal customs was suppressed. She answered to names like Annie, Patsy, and Lucinda, and her son was Ben, Amos, or Jim. The Negro was not given a surname because a surname identified family and by law the Negro had no family. Familial terms like mother, father, sister, and brother were prohibited. Any unauthorized use of these terms could result in flogging or worse.

The trauma associated with this experience made family formation extremely difficult. Even though the mothers held on to their tribal identity, the task of passing that identity on to a child was monumental. None of the tools required to instill tribal identity were available. She did not have the support of the child's father, her mother or father, sisters, brothers, uncles, aunts, cousins, elders, and friends. There was no village to help her raise her child. Not one remnant of African culture was visible, including dress, that could be shared with a child. Despite not having the tools they needed to transfer cultural identity, some women stood firm. They refused to impose Negro identity. Although captives in a strange land they stood their ground. But with all of their effort, their children only saw them as slaves. And because they were slaves the only sense of identity that they could communicate was that of race.

The children born under these conditions had no internal connection that was knowable. It could not be established because their parents were not in control. Slaves had no say in how the family was formed or how it operated.[6] The formation of the family was controlled exclusively by the master. Using this power, the internal connection with the family within was cut off. With the connection severed, the African could not live an internal life.

To live an internal life, Africans follow the customs and traditions of their ancestors, the most important being those that regulate family formation. There are numerous cultures found in Africa but they all have a common characteristic. To become viable, the formation of the family has to be controlled. Controlling family formation was the lifeblood of the African experience. The quality of life was determined by the quality of the family and the quality of the family was maintained by following customs. Among these customs one of the most important was marriage. To be recognized as a family in African society, marriage was essential. The decision to marry was left up to the individual but whom the individual married was decided by the family.

Most marriages were arranged between members of families that knew one another. If the families did not know one another, both families were notified and given ample time to undertake a vetting process. If either family was found to be objectionable the marriage did not take place.

The key to internal life is controlling the formation of the family. Having lost this power, children became the targets of a new aggressive push to infuse Negro identity. These children were not born into a traditional family; they were the byproducts of breeding. Breeders were not in business to produce families but to breed slaves to be sold. By law, slaves had no family. The law in the 1700s known as Slave Codes did not recognize kinship among slaves.

THE

AMERICAN SLAVE CODE

IN THEORY AND PRACTICE:

CHAPTER VII.
SLAVES CANNOT MARRY.

Being held as Property, and incapable of making any Contract, they cannot contract Marriage recognized by Law.

The slave has no rights. Of course he, or she, cannot have the rights of a husband, a wife. The slave is a chattel, and chattels do not marry. "The slave is not ranked among sentient beings, but among things," and things are not married.

"Slaves are not people, in the eye of the law."

CHAPTER VIII.
SLAVES CANNOT CONSTITUTE FAMILIES.

Being Property, "Goods" and "Chattels Personal," to all intents, constructions and purposes whatsoever, they have no claim on each other—no security from Separation—no Marital Rights— no Parental Rights—no Family Government—no Family Education— no Family Protection.

The family relation originates in the institution of marriage, and exists not without it. We have already proved that slaves cannot have families or be members of families, by proving that they cannot be married. To this latter point, in its connection with the former, we cite the words of Judge Jay:

"A *necessary consequence* of slavery is the absence of the marriage relation. No slave can commit bigamy, because the law knows no more of the marriage of slaves than of the marriage of brutes. A slave may, indeed, be formally married, but so far as legal rights and obligations are concerned, it is an idle ceremony." *Of course*, these laws do not recognize the *parental* relation, as belonging to slaves. A slave has no more legal authority over his child than a cow has over her calf.

The Family of Slaves

The union between a male and female slave that produced an offspring did not constitute a family.[7] The family of slaves had no legal standing. Family implied unity; any form of unity among slaves was thought to pose a threat. With this in mind every effort was made to prevent the slave family from forming. Marriage was not allowed and the use of familial terms such as mother, father, sister, and brother were forbidden. Any slave overheard using these terms was subjected to flogging or worst. These things were done to confound the slave population, in hopes that the threat of an organized rebellion would be eliminated. It was out of this chaotic environment that the Negro family emerged.

In terms of origin, the Negro family was unique in all the world. It had no legal status until slave owners gave in to the demands of the abolitionists to legitimize it. One of the main arguments against slavery was that it did not recognize the family of the slave. Slaves were treated the same as livestock. Responding to harsh criticism, slave owners gave up the practice of random breeding and allowed familial relationships to develop. Slaves could now use familial terms such as mother, father, sister, and brother and interact accordingly without fear of reprisal. Kinship among slaves was recognized and they were allowed to marry. For the first time, the slave family could claim an identity; that identity, however, was tied to the race.

The slave family had no power to fashion an identity. Although recognized as a legal entity, the owners controlled every aspect of family life. What appeared to be a family was in fact a charade. Nothing belonged to the slave. The slave had no say in how the family was formed or how it operated. The owner made all of the decisions related to family including what the family identity would be. Preserving white identity was the first consideration. To achieve this end, the identity of the slave family was tied to race. Race is the only identity the Negro family has known. No attempt has been made to forge a new identity. The same is true of the white family in America.

American culture does not allow the family to exist separately from race. This is not viewed as problematic because white identity keeps the white family on top. To hold on to the top position, the white family must live for the pleasure of the white race. The race is the ultimate beneficiary of everything the family does. The family belongs to the race. Everything the family accumulates represents the race and the possession that the family treasures most is whiteness.

Preserving white identity is about decorating the Racial Tree of Life. To decorate this tree there must be consumption. What the family consumes in terms of goods and services are placed on the Racial Tree of Life. Decorating the tree that represents the white race is responsible for American prosperity. The preservation of white identity is one of the driving forces that stimulates the American economy. Nothing the white family does contributes more to the preservation of white identity than what it consumes.

End Notes
Chapter Four

[1] Charles E. Kemper, ed. "The Calhoun Ancestry", <u>William and Mary Quarterly</u> [online] (1927) http://www.jstor.org/pss/1921317

[2] Dorothy Schneider & Carl J. Schneider, "An Eyewitness History of Slavery in America," <u>From Colonial Times to the Civil War</u> (Checkmark Books, 2001) 53.

[3] Schneider, 120.

[4] Schneider, 130.

[5] Schneider, 22.

[6] Schneider, 87.

[7] Schneider, 86.

5

Tying Race to Religion

I do not imagine that the white and black race will ever live in any country upon an equal footing. But I believe the difficulty to be still greater in the United States than elsewhere. An isolated individual may surmount the prejudices of religion, of his country, or of his race, and if this individual is a king he may effect surprising changes in society; but a whole people cannot rise, as it were, above itself. A despot who should subject the Americans and the former slaves to the same yoke, might perhaps succeed in commingling their races; but as long as the American democracy remains at the head of affairs no one will undertake so difficult a task; and it may be foreseen that the freer

the white population of the United States becomes, the more isolated will it remain.
—Alexis de Tocqueville, *Democracy in America* (1835)

The struggles of the African slaves in America is often compared to the struggles of the ancient Hebrew Israelites in Egypt.[1] Although there are many similarities, there is one detail that is often overlooked. No attempt was made by the Egyptians to strip the Hebrews of their identity. The Hebrew people were never forced to give up their names, their customs, and their culture to become a new people. The African experience in this regard is quite telling.

The African slave in America underwent a transformation like no other people in the history of mankind. The people who began their American journey as Africans became someone else along the way, they became Negroes. This never happened to the Hebrews or any other people. The repercussions from this transformation have never subsided.

Like the Hebrews, Negroes were also freed from their enslavement. The difference, however, is that the Negro has never found the "Promised Land." For 146 years since being emancipated, the Negro has been wandering around in the wilderness. The Hebrews took forty years to reach the "Promised Land," a distance of 250 miles that could have been covered in a matter of a month. Why did it take so long? Some surmise that the Hebrews were carrying excess baggage, in the form of a slave mentality.[2]

Like the Hebrew the Negro has assimilated a slave

mentality. Negroes don't trust and believe in themselves. They always seek the approval of the overseer. They place great value in the opinions of those who hover above them. The Negroes, like the Hebrews in the wilderness, lack self-respect and self-confidence. It was not until the Hebrews became devoid of this mentality that they were allowed to enter the "Promised Land."

The Negro mentality is a slave mentality. Like the Hebrew, the Negro is afraid to give it up because of a fear of the unknown. Negro identity is familiar and easy to master. The identity was constructed for those who are content with mediocrity. Religion was one of the most effective tools used to infuse Negro identity.[3] Given that race is a cultural construct, it is not surprising that the dominant force in western cultural life—Christianity—has exerted an enormous influence on its articulation. The book of Genesis has played a pivotal role in the cultural construction of race. Although many social and cultural factors have contributed significantly to western constructions of race, scripture has been for much of the early and modern eras the primary cultural influence of the forging of races. 'Race-as-theology' should be an important constituent of the humanistic study of racial constructs alongside accounts of 'race-as-biology', 'race-as-ethnicity', and race as class or caste.[4]

White Anglo Saxon Protestants

One of the first attempts to tie race to religion involved the use of the term White Anglo Saxon Protestants or WASP.

The redundant reference to white in this regard is quite telling. Anglo Saxons were white. There were no black Anglo Saxons, so why the repetition?

Over-accentuating white had two purposes. The principle purpose was to identify the top brass of the white race in America. This was not necessary in Europe; it only made sense in America where a culture of racial privilege was being erected. Within the white race there were two classes, the upper and lower class. To distinguish between them a term was coined, and that term was WASP. WASP identified the members of the upper class. There was no such term coined to identify the members of the lower class.

The secondary purpose was to take advantage of the dethronement of scripture from its dominant position in western intellectual life in the centuries following the Enlightenment. The decline in the authority of scripture opened up an ideological space for the uninhibited articulation of racialist sentiments giving life to external religion. Composed primarily of artisans and servants, the lower class for the most part was Catholic. The Catholic Church did not embrace the same racial theology that was practiced by the Protestants. This difference in theology was reflected in how immigrants to America were treated.[5] Catholic immigrants did not fare as well as Protestant, especially in the south. Of the 204 men given the title of Founding Father only three were Catholic. Perhaps Charles Carroll, the only Catholic signer of the Declaration of Independence, was brought into the fold because he was Maryland's largest slaveholder. Daniel Carroll, his cousin, and Thomas Fitzsimmons were the only Catholic signers of the Constitution. If a person was not a White Anglo Saxon Protestant, it was commonly understood that he or she was a member of the lower class even though that was not always true.

There were no White Anglo Saxon Catholics. Identifying with race before religion or ethnicity is a Protestant practice. It was not practiced in the Catholic Church where race and ethnicity had nothing to do with how a person was viewed spiritually. Unlike the Protestants, the Catholics immediately sought converts among African people as soon as they arrived in Africa. Although they took slaves, the slaves were baptized and given Christian surnames, a practice that was frowned upon by Protestants who after the Reformation refused to share their religion with people of another race.

The reluctance to share the Christian faith with the so-called Negro was not something new. The British were present in Africa for a hundred years before missionary activity began there. From its inception, Christianity was known as a proselytizing religion, its sacred and secular histories made manifest the necessity of bringing all non-Christians into the fold. Although the standard was clear, the tradition was ignored during Britain's initial African conquest. No effort was made by the British to convert Africans because they were feared to be possessed by demons.

Sir Thomas Herbert, a highly respected geographer, historian, and devout Protestant described Africans this way:

> **"[Negroes] in colour and so in condition are little more than Devils incarnate" and further "the Devil... has infused**

prodigious idolatry into their hearts, enough to relish his pallet and aggrandize their tortures when he gets power to fry their souls, as the raging sun has already scorched their cold black carcasses."

Herbert, like other early travelers to Africa, felt contempt for Africans. He was not inclined to share his faith with heathens. John Lok, another highly respected Englishman who traveled to Africa and brought four Africans back to England, had this to say about Africans: "They are people of beastly living, without a God, law, religion, or commonwealth." It was a hundred years before these sentiments changed. It was not until the late 17th century that the English took up serious missionary activity in Africa. America would later become the target of aggressive missionary activity.

At first, religion was met with great opposition, not only by slaves who were suspicious of the white man's religion, but also by the masters themselves who feared that any gathering of slaves might serve as a cloak for organized rebellion.[6] The slaveholders saw no benefit in saving the souls of their slaves. There was an ongoing debate, though not serious, about whether property actually had a soul.

When the Bishop of London inquired in 1724, "Are there any infidels, bond or free, within your Parish; and what means are used for their conversion?", he was met with a disappointing response: "Our Negro Slaves imported daily, are altogether ignorant of God and Religion, and in truth have so little Docility in them that they scarce ever become capable of Instruction; but… I have examined and improved several Negroes, Natives of Virginia" (*From James City Parish*). While the condition of the Negro's soul was questionable, the missionaries given charge of these souls were kept at bay by slaveholders.

There was a mounting fear of violent insurrection. To ward off missionary efforts by such groups as the Society for the Propagation of the Gospel, which had set up shop in London, laws were passed to minimize and control their activities. This law was passed in North Carolina in 1715:

> **"That if any master or owner of Negroes or slaves, or any other person or persons whatsoever in the government, shall permit or suffer any Negro or Negroes to build on their, or either of their lands, or any part thereof, any house under pretense of a meeting-house upon account of worship, or upon any pretense whatsoever, and shall not suppress and hinder them, he, she, or they so offending, shall, for every default, forfeit and pay fifty pounds, one-half towards defraying the contingent charges of the government, the other to him or them that shall sue for the same."**

In Maryland, a law was enacted in 1723 "to suppress tumultuous meetings of slaves on the Sabbath and other Holy days." In Georgia, constables were commanded to disperse any assembly or meeting of slaves" which may disturb or endanger the safety of His Majesty's subjects; and every slave which may be found at such a meeting may...

immediately be corrected, without trial, by receiving on the bare back twenty-five stripes, with a whip, switch or cow skin."

To protect their interest, every effort was made by slaveholders to suppress religious practices, both native and alien. These prohibitions, however, were reconsidered in the 1730s. A new religious movement known as the "Great Awakening" swept through the colonies in the 1730s. This new movement had its greatest impact on slaveholders, who were the primary target of the movement.[7] Slaveholders were convinced that they could strengthen their position as masters with their slaves by introducing religion. In fact, religion used properly could actually produce a happy, contented slave. Trying to take advantage of these new revelations while avoiding conflict with missionaries who were still feared at the time, the slave owners themselves became ministers. By the early 1750s, the majority of Southern slaveholders were ordained ministers.[8] They laid the foundation for what would later become Southern Fundamentalism.

Accepting Your Fate

It was from the pulpit that the slaveholder exercised his greatest power. As a messenger of God, he spoke on God's behalf. God's message to the slave was clear and simple: "Accept your fate." This theology of accepting one's fate was a reoccurring theme in sermons preached throughout the South by prominent Southern ministers who owned slaves.[9] The following is an excerpt from a sermon delivered by an unknown minister and slaveholder prior to the Civil War .[10]

"Every man must accept his fate. I must accept my fate and you must accept your fate. You were born a slave that was your fate. You were chosen by God, God wanted a slave and he chose you. God could have chosen me but instead he chose you. Does God make mistakes? God don't make mistakes if he made mistakes he wouldn't be God. I was born a master I didn't choose to be a master God made me a master that was my fate. God wanted a master for his slaves and he chose me. God is the master of our fate. He chose you to be a slave and he chose me to be your master. If we live this life according to our fate we will all be rewarded in the next life. This life is Gods preparation for the next. We should not try to change things that God has ordained.

When we take it upon ourselves to change what God has ordained, we defy Gods will. Bo defied Gods will when he ran away, didn't he? He refused to accept his fate he thought that freedom might make him happy, he was wrong. I want all of you to know that Bo aint happy. Bo aint happy because his heart is heavy, he knows he defied Gods will and he knows that he will be punished.

You can't be happy when you defy the will of God. In the 6th chapter of Ephesians verse five Gods says: "Slaves be obedient to your masters according to the flesh, with fear and trembling, in singleness of heart, as unto Christ." What does it mean to be obedient to your master in singleness of heart? The answer to this question is found in verse six where God says: "Not with eye service, as men pleasers; but as the servants of Christ, doing the will of God from the heart." Doing the will of God from the heart, what does that mean? It means you serve your master with love. In verse seven God says: "With good will doing service, as to the Lord and not to men." Listen hear God has made an arrangement. He has made an arrangement for you to serve him directly by serving me. Serving your master is no different than serving God. These are not my words these are Gods words. Listen to them again: "If you please your master you please God." What happens when we please God? Who knows what happens when you please God? I'll tell you what happens you get rewarded. Verse seven says: "Knowing that whatsoever good thing any man doeth, the same shall he receive of the Lord, whether he be bond or free."

In Gods eyes there is no difference between the slave and the master both are his servants. The slave's service and the master's service might appear to be different but in Gods eyes they are the same. Your master also has a master his master is

God. I must also please my master. I please my master by serving him. How do I serve him? I serve him by being a good master to you. We please God by serving him. I please him by being a good master and you please him by being a good slave. Good slaves are obedient they don't run away. Good slaves accept their fate they serve their master with love and devotion.

Are you obedient to your master? Are you serving him from the heart as if you were serving God? If not, you have not accepted your fate. You are defying Gods will and God will certainly punish you. God has given you a good master. Your master is a messenger of God. Serve your master well and God will certainly reward you."

Sermons like these were very persuasive. Hearing them from the master made them even more poignant, especially when he was holding the bible in one hand and a whip in the other. There were two ways for a slave to accept his fate, voluntarily or involuntarily. One way or the other, a slave had to submit.

To accept his fate voluntarily, the slave surrendered to his master and served him with love and devotion. For this kind of service the slave was rewarded.[11] After working from sun up to sun down for six days in blistering heat and freezing cold, he was given a day off. This day was celebrated as God's day, the Sabbath. It was a day for rest, reflection, and worship. On this day slaves could reflect on what it really meant to accept their fate. According to the master they were not only born slaves, they were also born Negroes. Did God create the Negro or was the Negro created by the master? Were Negroes creatures of divine nature or did they evolve from enmity? To create the illusion of a Godly derivation, the Negro was given the freedom to develop his own style of worship.

Negro Spirituals

No arena of life offered greater latitude for free expression to slaves than that found during religious observances. The West African traditions of chant, ritual, polyrhythm, and dance, long suppressed, were allowed to resurface along with the "ring shout" in a new resurrected form with Christian adaptation. Giving the Negro the freedom to craft his own style of worship turned out to be a brilliant psychological ploy. It produced what later became known as Negro Spirituals. Although the inspiration that created the genre came from people of different cultures, the credit for creating it was given to the race. Without the influence of European and West African cultures combined, there would be no Negro Spirituals.

Church music prior to the 1700s was confined to the singing of psalms at a snail's pace, without any instruments, in a "grave and serious" manner. British churchgoers were becoming increasingly dissatisfied with the dreary psalms as the only suitable means of praising God. Dr. Isaac Watts, a non-conformist, seized this opportunity to introduce "Hymns and Spiritual Songs" which were first published in 1707.[12]

Dr. Watts revolutionized church worship by introducing hymns. These new hymns were not dreary and bland, but lively and exuberant.[13] They contained engaging poetry that offered rest to the weary and deliverance to the captive. They reflected contemporary times with specific references to the poor and downtrodden. Watts was a counter-culturalist, at odds with the culture of oppression. His hymns sought to give hope, comfort, and strength to the oppressed.

Hearing these hymns the slaves were profoundly moved. The Watts spirituals were not only comforting; they were also rhythmic and boisterous. Some hymns dripped with emotion. The attraction they held for slaves led some to conclude that Watts did more to convert Africans to Protestant Christianity than anyone else. The Negro Spirituals were inspired by the "Hymns and Spiritual Songs" written by Dr. Watts. They are an outgrowth of a cultural tradition that he started.

Giving credit to the race for producing this unique cultural phenomenon was subterfuge designed to neuter cultural identity. The people who produced the genre did not identify themselves as Negroes. Their identity was rooted in ethnicity, not race. The Negro race only existed in the minds of whites and those who identified themselves as Negroes. Tying this cultural gem to race was part of a grand scheme to redefine culture. To shift the focus of identity, culture was tied to race. The word Negro identified a race of people; it did not identify a culture. At the time, the people who identified themselves as Negroes did not have a cultural identity. The key elements of culture, namely language and religion, were not products of Negro intellectual proficiency. The language was English and the religion was Christianity, neither of which was created by the Negro.

Because the Negro did not have a cultural identity, the advent of what became the Negro Spirituals presented an ideal opportunity to tie a cultural contribution to the race. Instead of giving credit to Dr. Watts and the West African tribes that created the genre, credit was given to the Negro race.[14] This set a precedent in terms of how Negro identity would evolve culturally.

According to this edict, any cultural offering produced by an African or European regardless of how the person identified himself belonged to his race. For the Negro this meant that he could not separate culture from race. The sovereignty of the race superseded all other claims. A Negro belonged to the race before he belonged to anything else, including God. His fate was determined by his race. Imposing this mindset turned religion on its head.

By tradition, religion had always been approached internally but for the Negro an external dimension was added. In this application, religion was used to tie God to the race. God's relationship with the race took precedent over His relationship with the family and the individual. Duped by this ruse, people were led to believe that God does not see them separate from their race. To receive His favor, the family and the individual had to be tied to the race. Embracing this understanding, the glorification of God took on a racial ambiance that could only manifest itself externally. This external spirituality did not allow an individual to separate himself from his race. Only within the confines of the race could God be worshiped. Two races could worship together but a distinction had to be made. It was by God's arrangement that one race was placed above another. To coexist peaceably it was incumbent that both races accept the positions that God had ordained. Tying God to race was not done to please God; it was done to preserve white identity. To achieve this end, religion was used to infuse Negro identity.

In 1805 when the importation of slaves was halted, more than fifty percent of the American slave population had been born in America. In 1867, right after the Civil War, there were some four million former slaves, all of them born in America. Thousands were interviewed and the findings were published in what are known as the Slave Chronicles. In all of the interviews there is not one account of any former slave identifying him or her self as anything other than Negro and Christian. And if taken to task, it's highly unlikely that anyone could have convinced them that they were not Negro and Christian. Negro was race and the religion tied to the Negro was Christianity.

Conditioned by the system, the Negro could not live outside of the race. To maintain Negro identity no one, black or white, was allowed to live beyond race. To preserve black identity, white identity had to also be persevered. One could not exist without the other. To claim the bottom position someone had to be on top. Whites were accepted on top because it gave the Negro a position in society. Being at the bottom was not so bad if you occupied the top position at the bottom.

On Top at the Bottom

Throughout out human history, there have always been those who take great comfort in knowing that there is someone beneath them. This sentiment was also found among the Negroes. How deeply these sentiments were held was revealed during the era of Negritude that began in the 1860s. In the early 1900s, under the crafty leadership of W. E. B. Dubois, a mulatto who identified himself as a Negro, class warfare at the bottom was initiated. Dubois was a gifted scholar, great orator, and one of the first black demagogues.[15] Like Jefferson, he considered race to be his single greatest attribute. It was Dubois, influenced by his ancestry, who recognized the hierarchy at the bottom. Referred to as the "Talented Tenth," these Negroes were heralded as the black equivalent to the White Anglo Saxon Protestant.

According to Dubois, it was their responsibility "to guide the mass away from the contamination and death of the worst in their race." Those who heeded his call were recruited as "Gate Keepers" by the white establishment. They were given the task of keeping those at the bottom of the bottom in their place. In doing so, the "Gate Keepers" could enjoy a position on top at the bottom. To perform this task, the "Gate Keepers" required education. The funds required to establish these institutions came from the White Anglo Saxon Protestant, who, by example, showed the importance of maintaining autonomy at the top.

There was power in division and Dubois understood it. Being at the bottom was not so bad if you were positioned on top of the bottom half. Having someone beneath you was quite comforting. Because this was his own experience, he was more interested in empowering the "Talented Tenth" than he was in empowering the masses. Those who benefited most from his work were those on top at the bottom. Because they were educated and enjoyed having someone beneath them, white America had no fear. Under no circumstances would "Gate Keepers" give up their positions.

Having secured the bottom positions, recruits were sought for the top positions. To increase the numbers at the top, Europeans were recruited with great enthusiasm. They played a prominent role in preserving white identity, but like the Africans and Native Americans, Europeans lived internal lives. External precepts such as race were not driving forces in their lives. Ethnicity, not race, was the principle source of identity. No one came to America cloaked in the garment of race. Working class immigrants to this country came with no racial animus in their hearts. It was not a part of their cultural makeup. They had no hatred for Native Americans or Africans. Most immigrants had no contact with either in their homeland. They knew themselves as belonging to a family and that's how they knew others. They saw no one separate from their family. Their first interaction with Native Americans and Africans was non-racial. Faced with the harrowing task of survival, there was no reason to harbor animosity towards anyone.

For the white elite, those who were born in America, this attitude was not welcomed. Being in the minority they feared that the working class might unite with the Negroes and Native Americans to overthrow them. To protect their interest they took up the task of erecting racial barriers. Among other things laws were passed that prohibited intermarriage. Some of the same strategies used to impose Negro identity on the African were used to impose white identity on British immigrants.

Although there were many similarities between African, Native American, and European societies there were also differences. African and Native American societies were less class oriented, which allowed a greater degree of closeness among its people. There was a distinct top and bottom in European society that kept the people divided. The class structure only allowed limited interaction between the upper and lower classes.

On the Bottom at the Top

Most of the immigrants who migrated to America belonged to the lower classes. These people had no history of being on top; the only position they knew was at the bottom.[16] After arriving in America things changed; for the first time they found people beneath them.

To enjoy a position at the top all they had to do was live for the pleasure of the race. Race was their ticket to the top. Their position at the top however was in the bottom half of the top. American society consisted of four tiers. The top position had two tiers, top and bottom and the bottom position had two tiers, top and bottom. The white lower classes occupied the bottom tier on top. From that position they could lord it over the Negro and Native American. This boost in status was by courtesy of the race. A debt was incurred in the process and that debt was expected to be repaid.

This was a new experience for those in the lower class who had only known ethnic identity. The opportunity to transition from ethnicity to race could not be done in their homeland. At the time, America was the only place on earth where people were rewarded for white skin. This was made possible by the presence of the Negro and Native American. Empowered by the state, anyone with white skin could enslave or even murder Negroes and Native Americans without fear of reprisal.

America was the land of liberty and one of the most coveted liberties was that which allowed the Negro and Native American to be brutalized to elevate the white race. No expression of whiteness was more telling than the gross inhumanity that occurred in the name of the race. Vicious acts of brutality were put on public display to rally the lower class.

The message was clear. There was no better way to express one's whiteness than to abuse a Negro or Native American. This mentality was encouraged and supported by Church Fathers who identified themselves as White Anglo Saxon Protestants. No institution took a more active role in promoting white supremacy than the Protestant Church. It was clearly articulated without any equivocation that "God favored the white race." Via the pulpit of the church the doctrine of white supremacy was spread throughout the land, and white identity was firmly ensconced by using an external form of religion that tied God to the race.

For the white lower class the message of white supremacy was one of liberation. For the first time they could experience what it was like to be members of the upper class. To be favored, it did not matter what family they hailed from; all they had to do was live for the pleasure of the race. Living for the white race was no different than living for God; the two were tied together.

Not everyone who came in contact with this theology was gullible enough to believe it. Contrary to popular belief, America did not become a racist caldron overnight. The whitewashing of America took place gradually. There were those who had white skin that were not interested in living for the race. Nothing could convince them to give up their ethnic identity to become a white devotee. John Brown was one of these great American heroes.

Instead of stepping on black folks Brown preferred to lift them up, and for doing so his life was put into peril. No Americans have a more illustrative history of loving and giving than the abolitionists. Without their courageous efforts the Negro might still be enslaved. What they did, they did for the sake of humanity, not for the sake of the race. Their biggest detractors were members of their own race. Unwavering in their zeal and determination, they totally dismantled the evil institution of slavery.

Men with white skin freed the Negro to the dismay of their bigoted brethren. Their contribution to the cause of freedom, although unsurpassed, has never gotten just acclaim, not even from those they freed. The appropriate appreciation has not been forthcoming because the Negro is not his own being. He belongs to the race. The race cannot show gratitude because the race is bound in shackles that have not been completely removed because too many people, black and white, benefit from keeping them in place.

End Notes
Chapter Five

[1] Eddie S. Glaude, Exodus!: Religion, Race and Nation in Early Nineteenth Century Black America (Chicago: University of Chicago Press, 2000) 3.

(2) Dr. Rabbi Stuart W. Gershon, "Those Who Get To Enter The Promised Land Are Those Who Overcome Their Fear" [online] 2008, www.templesinainj.org/contentsermons/pdf/2008-06-20. Sermon.pdf

(3) Colin Kidd, The Forging of Races, Race and Scripture in the Protestant Atlantic World, 1600–2000 (Oxford: Cambridge University Press, 2006) 19.

(4) Kidd, 20.

(5) John B. Boles, Masters & Slaves in the House of the Lord (Lexington: University of Kentucky Press, 1990) 127.

(6) Kidd, 24.

(7) Kidd, 19-20.

(8) Elizabeth Fox-Genovese & Eugene D. Genovese, The Mind of the Master Class: History and Faith in the Slave Holders World View (Oxford: Cambridge University Press, 2005) 490.

(9) Duncan J. MacLeod, Slavery, Race, and the American Revolution (Oxford: Cambridge University Press, 2008) 24.

(10) Rev. H. Caldwell, Slavery and Southern Methodism: Two Sermons Preached in the Medothist Church in Newman, Georgia [online] (1865) www.archive.org

(11) Theresa A. Singleton, I Too, Am America (Charlottesville: University of Virginia Press, 1999) 223–224.

(12) Viv Broughton, Black Gospel: An Illustrated History of the Gospel (London: Sterling Publishing Co., 1985).

(13) Robert Southley, Isaac Watts, Biography (Christian Biography Resources, New York: Little Brown & Company, 1834).

(14) John Lovell, Black Song: The Forge and the Flame, The Story of How the Afro-American Spiritual Was Hammered Out (New York: Macmillian 1972) 71.

(15) W. E. B. DuBois, "The Talented Tenth" [online] (1903) www.yale.edu.glc.archive/1148.htm

(16) Jim Goad, The Redneck Manifesto (New York: Simon & Schuster, 1998) 15.

6

The Deification of Race

Perceptual Reality

Humans are the only creatures on earth that assimilate identity. The identity we assimilate, determines our perceptual reality, the place from whence we project our identity. Since prehistoric times, that place was internal and the identities projected were family, religion, and culture. These identities were given life by developing the fundamentals that define them. To develop these fundamentals, intelligence and ingenuity were required. Let's take culture for instance.

Fledgling cultures came to life when the leaders applied advanced intellect to create systems of language, justice, diet, economics, architecture, agriculture, medicine, education, self-defense, art, science, and music. Only after the fundamentals were developed did the people have a culture to identify with. The same was true for family and religion. Among the fundamentals that gave life to family identity was the recognition of kin. Terms were coined to identify each family member according to how they were related to one another. A man could be related as a son, father, grandfather, uncle, brother, nephew, and cousin. A woman could be related as daughter, mother, grandmother, aunt, sister, niece, and cousin. Other fundamentals that gave life to family identity were customs and traditions. Among these customs and traditions were the celebration of weddings, conceptions, births, first tooth, anniversaries, and the coming of age.

Religion was also given life by fundamentals found in the scriptures. Among them are precepts such as "Love the Lord thy God with all thy heart and soul," and "Love thy neighbor as thy self." Throughout history the identities people assimilated were supported by fundamentals. This was true until America's founding. Americans did what no other people had ever done. They assimilated an identity that had no fundamentals. Race is an external construct that is based solely on physical attributes. There are no fundamentals to support race. It cannot stand on its own. To be given life, race had to be tied to something concrete such as family, religion, and culture. Tying race to family, religion, and culture, America produced one of the most corrupt societies in the history of mankind. Because of its sinister nature, everything tied to race becomes corrupt. The motivation that produced the concept was corrupt.

American society was corrupted by projecting images of race on all its people. The device used to fix these images was the census. Before the census was taken, the family, religion, and culture of the immigrants was not tied to race. Their perceptual reality was internal. To change the paradigm, Thomas Jefferson and his cohorts used the census. The census is an external device that fixes racial identity. How you identified yourself did not matter; the census had the final say. Using this device, Jefferson was able to assemble a multitude of races.

The Idol of the Race

Acting as the "High Priest of the White Race," Jefferson presided over the ceremony that brought to life the most powerful idol in the history of the world. The people involved in this initiation were not aware that they were worshiping. Even though they were asked to offer their thoughts, deeds, emotions, dreams, intellect, culture, and family to the race, it never occurred to them that it was worship. Not revealing this is perhaps the greatest act of deception ever performed.

Even though Jefferson initiated the worship, he should not be blamed for this outrage. After all, race was the only identity that he knew. Although well educated and extremely intelligent, he knew nothing of internal life. Considering his background, it's highly unlikely that he even realized what he was doing.

Among idols the white race is the most pervasive ever contrived. The worshipers are the mouths, eyes, ears, nose, tongue, hands, arms, belly, legs, feet, mind, heart, and soul of the deity. Because the idol is also the worshiper, it can be in a thousand different places simultaneously, spreading its influence and advancing its cause. Jefferson spoke the idol of the white race into existence. In the same breath he created a permanent underclass consisting of blacks and Native Americans. In the following exposé,[1] Jefferson detailed the inferiority of the black race:

> **"It will probably be asked, Why not retain and incorporate the blacks into the state, and thus save the expense of supplying, by importation of white settlers, the vacancies they will leave? Deep rooted prejudices entertained by the whites; ten thousand recollections, by the blacks, of the injuries they have sustained; new provocations; the real distinctions which nature has made; and many other circumstances, will divide us into parties, and produce convulsions, which will probably never end but in the extermination of the one or the other race. - To these objections, which are political, may be added others, which are physical and moral. The first difference which**

strikes us; is that of colour. - Whether the black of the negro resides in the reticular membrane between the skin and scarf-skin, or in the scarf-skin itself; whether it proceeds from the colour of the blood, the colour of the bile, or from that of some other secretion, the difference is fixed in nature, and is as real as if its seat and cause were better known to us. And is this difference of no importance? Is it not the foundation of a greater or less share of beauty in the two races? Are not the fine mixtures of red and white, the expressions of every passion by greater or less suffusions of colour in the one, preferable to that eternal monotony, which reigns in the countenances, that immovable veil of black which covers all the emotions of the other race? Add to these, flowing hair, a more elegant symmetry of form, their own judgment in favour of the whites, declared by their preference of them, as uniformly as is the preference of the Oranootan for the black women over those of his own species. The circumstance of Superior beauty, is thought worthy attention in the propagation of our horses, dogs, and other domestic animals; why not in that of man? Besides those of colour, figure, and hair, there are other physical distinctions proving a difference of race. They have less hair on the face and body. They secrete less by the kidneys, and more by the glands of the skin, which gives them a very strong and disagreeable odour. This greater degree of transpiration renders them more tolerant of heat, and less so of cold than the whites. Perhaps too a difference of structure in the pulmonary apparatus, which a late ingenious experimentalist has discovered to be the principal regulator of animal heat, may have disabled them from extricating, in the act of inspiration, so much of that fluid from the outer air, or obliged them in expiration, to part with more of it. They seem to require less sleep. A black after hard labour through the day, will be induced by the slightest amusements to sit up till midnight, or later, though knowing he must be out with the first dawn of the morning. They are at least as brave, and more adventuresome. But this may perhaps proceed from a want of forethought, which prevents their seeing a danger till it be present. - When present, they do not go through it with more coolness or steadiness than the whites. They are more ardent after their female: but love seems with them to be more an eager desire, than a tender delicate mixture of sentiment and sensation. Their griefs are transient.

Those numberless afflictions, which render it doubtful whether heaven has given life to us in mercy or in wrath, are less felt, and sooner forgotten with them. In general, their existence appears to participate more of sensation than reflection. To this must be ascribed their disposition to sleep when abstracted from their diversions, and unemployed in labour. An animal whose body is at rest, and who does not reflect, must be disposed to sleep of course. Comparing them by their faculties of memory, reason, and imagination, it appears to me that in memory they are equal to the whites; in reason much inferior, as I think one could scarcely be found capable of tracing and comprehending the investigations of Euclid; and that in imagination they are dull, tasteless, and anomalous. It would be unfair to follow them to Africa for this investigation.

When Thomas Jefferson wrote these words neither race, black nor white, was consolidated. There were only a few men at the time that identified themselves as white males. The evolution of white identity was not instantaneous, as a popular myth would have us believe. The whitewashing of America was a gradual process that succeeded over time. It was influenced by two major factors: the lack of a tangible cultural identity and the presence of slaves, the latter being the greatest contributor.

Peter Jefferson, the father of Thomas Jefferson, owned slaves and identified himself as a white male. As a child, his son Thomas found himself from time to time in the arms of a woman with a black face. Interacting with blacks was a part of the daily routine that shaped his perceptual reality.

This scenario was repeated in the lives of James Madison, James Monroe, and most of the other Founding Fathers. Seeing black faces while growing up was a common occurrence for a white child and it was not long before these sons of privilege understood that the black faces belonged to Negroes and that Negroes were members of an inferior race. To justify their enslavement, Peter Jefferson told his son, "Slaves have black faces and are inferior to whites. If you study the slave with your own eyes you will see what I mean." As was revealed in his writings, Jefferson began his study of Negroes in his youth. Put at ease by familiarity, it never occurred to him that the people he was studying had been conditioned by their confinement. What they understood to be a Negro was limited to what they were allowed to experience. That experience was structured to produce an inferior human being.

How credible is a study whose purpose is to prove your superiority and thus justify enslavement? How could you possibly conclude that someone you own is your equal? Thomas Jefferson, like his slaves, lived for the race. Living for the race as a slave was not the same as living for the race as the master. The interaction he observed did not take place on a level playing field. The whites were on top and the blacks were at the bottom. Everyday he saw with his own eyes white superiority put on display. By observing the interaction between the races Jefferson learned how to think, act, and speak as a superior. He was conditioned by his experience to see life through the eyes of the race. He was not born with this predisposition he was inured by the environment he grew up in. To become a white male he tied his thoughts, deeds, emotions, dreams, intellect, family, and his God to the white race. He did so without reservations or regrets. Viewing life through the eyes of race, he could not see beyond race. The racial mindset he imbibed was all-pervasive, which made him uniquely qualified to disseminate race on behalf of the government of the United States.

Jefferson was authorized by the government to take a census. With this authorization he was empowered to impose race. The race he imposed was two-dimensional. It consisted of an identity and a space. What identity and space you received was determined by the color of your skin. If your skin was white, you were issued white identity and allocated space at the top. If your skin was dark, you were issued Negro identity and allocated space at the bottom. The identity you received was fashioned in the form of a brooch.

The Brooch of Racial Identity

Thomas Jefferson was America's first brooch maker. Using the census, a tool created by James Madison, Jefferson crafted brooches for everyone in America at the time. These brooches were decorative ornaments worn in the mind that tied individuals to their race. Jefferson made beautiful brooches for whites and hideous brooches for blacks and Native Americans. The distribution of the brooches took place during the taking of the census.

Everyone who took the census was issued a brooch and assigned a space. Whites occupied the space on top. No class distinctions were made. This was done to consolidate the race. After the Revolutionary War, the separation between the upper and lower class had not changed. Freedom had no impact on the class structure of society. The upper and lower class did not share the same space. To consolidate the race, a device was needed to draw the upper and lower class together and thus eliminate class.

Eliminating class by sharing wealth equally within the race was not an option. What Jefferson did instead was raise the status of lower class whites by creating a new lower class consisting of Negroes and Native Americans. For the first time lower class whites found someone beneath them. In accordance to the census all whites were assigned the same space. The census made it no longer necessary for the upper and lower classes to occupy different space.

Wearing the white brooch of racial identity, members of the lower class could sit at the same table as the white elite. The brooches they wore were identical. Although issued to everyone, black or white, not everyone was pleased with the brooch. There were those who took issue with a system that imposed identity on them. When it was first offered to Africans, the brooch was rejected. Why would anyone in their right minds agree to be identified as members of a permanent underclass?

Considering the implications, it is not at all surprising that innocent children were the first to accept the brooch of Negro identity. Children are quite vulnerable, especially children held as chattel slaves. Considering this, it's not difficult to understand why they were the first to don the brooch of racial identity and utter the words, "I am a Negro." These words were uttered out of ignorance, without a true understanding of what they meant. But having worn the brooch, the Negro has never taken it off, even after realizing its sinister nature.

Jefferson also allocated space to the Negro. This space was positioned at the bottom. It was never intended to be permanent. It might best be described as a temporary labor camp. The slaves who occupied the black reservation were thought to be temporary workers. After they built the "Great White Society," they were to be sent back home to their native land. In Jefferson's mind assimilating Negroes into American culture was unthinkable. As human beings they were inferior, their worth was calculated only in terms of their labor. Free labor.

> "My opinion on the proposition… to take measures for procuring on the coast of Africa, an establishment to which the people of color of these States might, from time to time, be colonized, under the auspices of different governments [is]: Having long ago made up my mind on this subject, I have no hesitation in saying that I have ever thought it the most desirable measure which could be adopted for gradually drawing off this part of our population, most advantageous for themselves as well as for us. Going from a country possessing all the useful arts, they might be the means of transplanting them

among the inhabitants of Africa, and would
thus carry back to the country of their
origin the seeds of civilization which might
render their sojournment and sufferings
here a blessing in the end to that country."
–Thomas Jefferson to John Lynch, 1811.
ME 13:10

The difference between white space and black space was like night and day. The space allocated to Negroes was no different than the space that was set aside for domestic animals—the field, the sty, the pen, the barn, and the stable. This space was unfit for human habitation and did not belong to the Negro. The Negro did not own anything, including his person. He was property and property had no rights or possessions. The Negro had no authority to control the space that was allocated to him. Only those with white faces could regulate Negro space. The space was structured to dehumanize the occupant. The language, the diet, and the religion were all vitiated. It was in this space that the Negro came to know racial domination. It was from the position of racial dominance that Thomas Jefferson issued his mandates.

In all fairness however, I would be amiss, if I did not mention the fact that he did speak ill of the institution that he willfully participated in.

"Nothing is more certainly written
in the book of fate than that these people
[blacks] are to be free. Nor is it less certain
that the two races, equally free, cannot
live in the same government. Nature,

habit, opinion has drawn indelible lines of distinction between them."
    –Thomas Jefferson: Autobiography, 1821.
    ME 1:72

Jefferson spoke eloquently about abolishing the institution of slavery but in his lifetime did not free one slave. Neither did he retract his statements regarding the inferiority of the black race. Jefferson cloaked himself in the dress of a reformer but his words did not match his deeds. Assisted by the other Founders he created a living hell for Negroes. His grand scheme to end slavery by shipping Negroes back to Africa was not implemented on his watch. During his presidency from 1801 to 1810, not one slave was shipped back to Africa. There was little or no change on the black reservation until emancipation came.

Appalled by the horrible conditions found in black space, abolitionist such as John Brown stood up to oppose the status quo. Brown, taking defiance to a new level, opted to resort to violence. His courageous stand was perhaps the spark that ignited the Civil War. Although the cause of the war has been hotly debated, one thing cannot be denied: it improved the condition of black space. Thanks to Abraham Lincoln, Negroes for the first time took ownership of the space they were allocated. Instead of being forced to live for the race, the Negro people were given an opportunity to choose a new identity. This amazing turn of events, as fate would have it, was very short-lived.

The Train to Freedom

After centuries of waiting, emancipation, the much anticipated "Train to Freedom," finally arrived at the station. Shortly after leaving the station, the train was sidetracked by the "Black Codes." Employed to impede human development, the issuance of the Black Codes was a desperate attempt to maintain control of black space. As this North Carolina law illustrates, maintaining control was done, by keeping people in ignorance.

> *"Any free person, who shall teach, or attempt to teach, any slave to read or write, the use of figures excepted, or shall give or sell to such slave any book or pamphlet, shall be deemed guilty of a misdemeanor, if a white man or woman, shall be fined not less than one hundred nor more than two hundred dollars, or imprisoned, and if a free person of colour, shall be fined, imprisoned, or whipped not exceeding thirty-nine nor less than twenty lashes."*
> –North Carolina Black Codes

Control of black space was relinquished but was taken back in a power grab just months after Lincoln's assassination. The specter of unregulated Negro space sent shivers through the spines of white demagogues. To put an end to this outrage, new laws were passed that imposed severe restrictions on freed slaves, such as:

> *Prohibiting their right to vote, forbidding them to sit on juries, limiting their right*

to testify against white men, carrying weapons in public places and working in certain occupations.

These laws were supported by the then president, Andrew Johnson who made these remarks to Thomas C. Fletcher, the governor of Missouri at the time:

"This is a country for white men, and by God, as long as I am President, it shall be a government for white men."

His views on racial equality were clearly defined in a letter to Benjamin B. French, the Commissioner of Public Buildings:

"Everyone would, and must admit, that the white race was superior to the black, and that while we ought to do our best to bring them up to our present level, that, in doing so, we should, at the same time raise our own intellectual status so that the relative position of the two races would be the same."

After being derailed by the Black Codes, the "Freedom Train" was put back on track by the Civil Rights Act of 1866:

The act declared that all persons born in the United States were now citizens, without regard to race, color, or previous condition.

As citizens they could make and enforce contracts, sue and be sued, give evidence in court, and inherit, purchase, lease, sell, hold, and convey real and personal property. Persons who denied these rights to former slaves were guilty of a misdemeanor and upon conviction faced a fine not exceeding $1,000, or imprisonment not exceeding one year, or both.

To provide even more security, both houses passed the Fourteenth Amendment to the Constitution in 1866. This Amendment was designed to grant citizenship to and protect the civil liberties of recently freed slaves. It did this by prohibiting states from denying or abridging the privileges or immunities of citizens of the United States, depriving any person of his life, liberty, or property without due process of law, or denying to any person within their jurisdiction the equal protection of the laws.

Most of the Southern states refused to ratify the Fourteenth Amendment, and in response Congress passed the Reconstruction Act in 1867. The South was divided into five military districts, each under a major general. New elections were to be held in each state with freed male slaves being allowed to vote. The act also included an amendment that offered readmission to the Southern states after they had ratified the Fourteenth Amendment. This amendment was enacted to secure Negro space. It was the government's guarantee that space allocated to the Negro would be controlled exclusively by the Negro. Powered by the Reconstruction Act, the "Freedom Train" sped down the tracks towards total equality.

The Ku Klux Klan

In 1867, one year after the Fourteenth Amendment was ratified, in the name of Almighty God, Nathan Bedford Forest, the second "High Priest of the White Race," founded the Ku Klux Klan. The Klan is a Christian organization that is dedicated to preserving the supremacy of the white race. The Charter of the organization reads thus:

> THIS IS A WHITE CHRISTIAN ORGANIZATION, exalting the Caucasian Race and teaching the doctrine of white pride. This does not mean that we are enemies of the colored and mongrel races. But it does mean that we are organized to establish the solidarity and to realize the mission of the White Race. All of Christian Civilization depends upon the preservation and up building of the White Race, and it is the mission of the Ku Klux Klan to proclaim this doctrine until the White Race shall come into its own. THIS IS A WHITE CHRISTIAN ORGANIZATION, for and about Gods Chosen People, and as such has as its mission the interpretation of the highest ideals of the White, peoples.

IDEALS: WE STAND FOR WHITE CHRISTIAN VALUES.

Distinction among the races is not accidental but designed. This is clearly brought out in the

Bible the one book that tells authoritatively of the origin of the races. This distinction is not incidental, but is of the vastest importance and indicates the wisdom of the divine mind. It is not temporary but is as binding as the ages that have not yet ceased to roll. The Pride of the White Race must be maintained or be overwhelmed by the rising tide of color and the special rights and privileges so easily afforded to those of minority status. WE MUST KEEP THIS A FREE COUNTRY. Only by doing this, can we be faithful to the foundations laid by our forefathers.

The race worship espoused by Thomas Jefferson was purely political and was inspired by economics. It was not tied to religion directly. Jefferson may have sown the seeds but he never used God to justify the worship of the white race. His was a secular doctrine that was not based on any religious precept.

The Klan was the first organization in America to use God to justify worshiping the white race. How you worshipped the race was left open to interpretation; the common objective, however, was keeping the Negro down. There were numerous ways the Klan found to perform its sacred rites, all of which involved some form of obstruction. They included the obstruction of education, the right to vote, freedom of assembly, equal justice under the law, employment, and the ultimate obstruction, the taking of the Negro's life. To please the idol of the white race, Negroes were murdered. When it came to advancing the race nothing was put off limits, all of which was done in the name of Jesus Christ.

Jim Crow

After being terrorized for ten years by the enactment of the Black Codes and Jim Crow laws, the "Train to Freedom" was derailed. The obsession with controlling Negro space had not gone away; it resurfaced in the form of segregation. By law, whites could not control Negro space internally, as they once did. The only control that could be exercised was external. Jim Crow was an attempt to do just that. A wall was built around the white reservation. Negroes were not allowed to own property. Their only excuse for being there was to work. Separate accommodations were provided in all public places. Entry for the Negro was always in the rear. White only institutions such as clubs, schools, colleges, universities, and churches, were established to ensure that the Negro was kept at bay.

Jim Crow was the name of the racial caste system that operated primarily, but not exclusively, in the Southern and Border States between 1877 and the mid-1960s. The Jim Crow system was under-girded by the following beliefs or rationalizations: whites were superior to blacks in all important ways, including but not limited to intelligence, morality, and civilized behavior; sexual relations between blacks and whites would produce a mongrel race which would destroy America; treating blacks as equals would encourage interracial sexual unions; any activity which suggested social equality encouraged interracial sexual relations; if necessary, violence must be used to keep blacks at the bottom of the racial hierarchy. The following Jim Crow etiquette norms show how inclusive and pervasive these norms were:

a. A black male could not offer his hand (to shake hands) with a white male because it implied being socially equal. Obviously, a black male could not offer his hand or any other part of his body to a white woman, because he risked being accused of rape.

b. Blacks and whites were not supposed to eat together. If they did eat together, whites were to be served first, and some sort of partition was to be placed between them.

c. Under no circumstance was a black male to offer to light the cigarette of a white female —that gesture implied intimacy.

d. Blacks were not allowed to show public affection toward one another in public, especially kissing, because it offended whites.

e. Jim Crow etiquette prescribed that blacks were introduced to whites, never whites to blacks. For example: "Mr. Peters (the white person), this is Charlie (the black person), that I spoke to you about."

f. Whites did not use courtesy titles of respect when referring to blacks, for example, Mr., Mrs., Miss, Sir, or Ma'am. Instead, blacks were called by their first names. Blacks had to use courtesy titles when referring to whites, and were not allowed to call them by their first names.

g. If a black person rode in a car driven by a white person, the black person sat in the back seat, or the back of a truck.

h. White motorists had the right of way at all intersections.

Stetson Kennedy, the author of Jim Crow Guide, offered these simple rules that blacks were supposed to observe in conversing with whites:

a. Never assert or even intimate that a White person is lying.
b. Never impute dishonorable intentions to a White person.
c. Never suggest that a White person is from an inferior class.
d. Never lay claim to, or overly demonstrate, superior knowledge or intelligence.
e. Never curse a White person.
f. Never laugh derisively at a White person.
g. Never comment upon the appearance of a White female.

It was during the Jim Crow era that the worship of the white race reached its pinnacle. The Negro was given a significant role to play in the worship of the white race. As the subject of human sacrifices, the Negro knew first hand how serious the worshipers of the white race were. Nothing pleased the idol of the white race more than the lynching of a Negro.

The High Priest of the Black Race

In response to this carnage, a black Thomas Jefferson rose up from the ashes in the person of Marcus Garvey. Garvey took up the hideous brooch of Negro identity and wore it as his breastplate. He refused to sit by idly and do nothing. To stop the wholesale desecration of the Negro people, he founded the Universal Negro Improvement Association (UNIA). The first movement for Black Nationalism, the mission of UNIA was to liberate the black race. To realize his dream, Garvey put forth the following proposal:

Declaration of Rights of the Negro Peoples of the World Universal Negro Improvement Association and African Communities League (UNIA-ACL) (1887-1940)

Drafted and adopted at the Convention held in New York, 1920, over which Marcus Garvey presided as Chairman, and at which he was elected Provisional President of Africa.

PREAMBLE

Be it Resolved, That the Negro people of the world, through their chosen representatives in convention assembled in Liberty Hall, in the City of New York and United States of America, from August 1 to August 31, in the year of our Lord, one thousand nine hundred and twenty, protest against the wrongs and injustices they are suffering at the hands of their white brethren, and state what

they deem their fair and just rights, as well as the treatment they propose to demand of all men in the future.

Garvey was a well-intended man who responded to whiteness the only way he knew how—with blackness. After taking up the brooch, he did what Jefferson hoped he would do: encourage others to take it up and wear it proudly. A great writer and orator, Garvey was the black Thomas Jefferson of his day. He not only took up the brooch of Negro identity; he dispensed it throughout the world. Although never formally recognized, Garvey assumed the role of the first "High Priest of the Black Race." He did for black identity what Jefferson did for white.

Garvey rose to the top overnight and fell even faster. The mantel of leadership he established however was never abandoned. It was passed on to the Honorable Elijah Muhammad, the second "High Priest of the Black Race."

When Elijah entered the scene, blacks were on their backs suffering from severe cardiac arrest caused by Jim Crow laws and the Great Depression. To bring the people back to life, Elijah used what some have described as a defibrillator. His teachings were in some minds like electrical shock treatment. Those who underwent the treatment were given new life, life as a Muslim.

Elijah took up the brooch of Negro identity and led the people in a new direction. Like Garvey, he saw blacks as the living dead, shadows of the white man. In a statement about why blacks have a problem with identity, Elijah said, "Blacks want to be everything but themselves. They want to be white men. They process their hair. Act like white men. They want to integrate with the white man but cannot integrate himself with his own kind. The Negro wants to lose his identity because he does not know his own identity." To be liberated he believed that the Negro had to change his behavior. To do that, he would have to give up his association with white men. In Elijah's mind the white man was the devil.

Unable to deny the success enjoyed by the White Anglo Saxon Protestants who introduced race to Christianity, Elijah following their example and introduced race to Islam. Using his keen intellect and wit, he fashioned a new image of the Negro and placed it on an altar to be worshiped. Under the guise of religion he initiated the first worship of the black race. According to Elijah, it was Allah who authorized this worship. This revelation was explained in his teachings:

> **"The black people in America are, by nature, born Muslim. The enemy slave-making devil, deprived the Black Man in America of the knowledge of himself. The Black man in America has a wonderful chance to be set in Heaven at once. And not in Hell If he will accept the opportunity by accepting Islam. Islam is the nature in which the Black man was created. The Black Man was created in the nature of righteousness and not in the nature of evil. I do not care what you say about the Black man he is not an evil man, by nature, The black man is good, by nature, and all you have to do is strip**

off that which is not himself. The Black Man being born under and nursed by the enemy. The enemy will make you to be like he would like you to be. This is what has happened to us, the black man in America. Just think of how much love the Black man and the Black Woman has for the white people. You can hardly get the Black man on the road to self. The road to self is an unlimited road, But the white man has fascinated the Black Man with wealth and luxury and the Black Man is not looking to do anything for self. He wants his self in the white man, just for the sake of temporary luxury. They are satisfied just to work for the smile and the look of friendship of white people."

As the "High Priest of the Black Race," Elijah Muhammad spoke on behalf of Allah. According to Elijah, "Allah favored black men over white." The key to black liberation was to worship the black race. The black race is righteous and worthy of worship. Turn away from the idol of the white race. This was the message espoused by the Honorable Elijah Muhammad. He said, "The white race is being worshiped in the form of Jesus Christ. Christianity has not gotten you anywhere, it keeps you tied to the white man. Turn away from the white devils and worship your own kind."

In Defense of Black and White

In response to Elijah Muhammad's "Message to the Black Man in America," J. B. Stoner, the third "High Priest of the White Race" and leader of the Ku Klux Klan, wrote this letter in 1956:

> 1 Thessalonians 2:14-16 St. John 8:44-48
>
> **CHRISTIAN KNIGHTS of the KU KLUX KLAN**
>
> **Archleader, J.B. Stoner, P.O. Box 48 Imperial Wizard Atlanta, Ga.**
>
> **Infidels:**
>
> **Repent of Mohammedanism or burn in hell forever, throughout eternity.**
>
> **Islam is a product of the colored race. Islam is a dark religion for dark people. I don't know why Africans would support Islam for any other reason except of race. There are several reasons why niggers should oppose it. One reason is that the Qur-an forbids Muslims to drink intoxicating drinks, whereas most niggers like to get drunk. It says also that thieves should have their hands cut off. How many niggers would be left with hands?**

Christianity, the one and only true religion, has only been successful in white nations among white people, as recognized in the literature of the Christian Party. Christianity prevails in every white nation, even when outlawed, but does not appear to have roots in any colored nation that could withstand tribulation. Therefore on a racial group basis, it would appear that only the superior white race is capable of appreciating Christianity and that the dark inferior races prefer a heathen religion like Islam. Therefore, it is obvious that we Christians should work hard to preserve the great white race.

ONLY WHITE WOMEN ARE BEAUTIFUL

One of the main purposes of Mohammedan invasion of white Europe was to capture white women. Only white women are beautiful. When ruling over white sections of Europe, part of the tribute required of the conquered people was the regular giving of beautiful white women to the Muslims as slaves. They didn't like their own dark women. The African race has never produced a beautiful woman so the Muslims were naturally not satisfied with their own black women. If the Africans were as good as whites, they would be happy with their own women instead of lusting for our white women. Your desire for white women is an admission of your own racial inferiority. One reason why we whites will never accept you into our white society is because a nigger's chief ambition in life is to sleep with a white woman thereby polluting her. Every time a demented white woman marries a nigger, your newspapers brag about the sin. The day will come when no nigger will be allowed to even look at a white woman or a white woman's picture. That will be a sad day for the men of your race who have no respect for their own women won't it? For your information, nigger is the Latin word for black, so why are you ashamed of it?

YOU WANT WHITE BLOOD PUMPED INTO YOUR RACE

Yes, Africans in America are ashamed of their own race. They regret that they are what they are. As proof, look at the nigger newspaper that advertise skin whiteners, and so-called hair straighteners. If blacks are as good as whites why aren't they proud of their black skins and the kinky wool on top of their heads? If you aren't ashamed of your race, why don't you strive to keep it pure and preserve it and its characteristics?

You blacks have a lower opinion of your own race than we whites have. You hate, yes hate your own African race so much that you want to destroy it by mixing your blood with white blood. You want white blood pumped into your race **because you think white blood is better** and will improve you and make you less Negroid, less African. You are trying to forget your heritage and your race by associating with your white superiors.

If you were as good as whites and equal to us, you would not be trying to force yourselves into white society. You would be happy with the company of your fellow Africans. Or, is the odor too much for you? Since you niggers don't respect your own race and don't love your race enough to preserve it, how can you expect white people to respect it? I have more respect for an African who believes in Black Supremacy and racial purity than I do for an African who hates his own race and tries vainly to disown it. I admire the African who says that no white man is good enough to shake hands with him.

SEGREGATION

I hope you will appreciate the fact that I am not a hypocrite like some Yankees who preach race-mixing and practice segregation. I actually express the sentiments and feelings that are in the hearts of most white people everywhere when I tell you that I believe in white supremacy and the inferiority of all dark races.

Why should we whites let Africans infiltrate our civilization when Africans have never been able to build or maintain a civilization of their own? You Africans are afraid to do it alone. You are afraid that you would get lost without the white man to guide you and help you. Yet with your mania for mongrelization, you are trying to destroy the white race that has given you civilization on a silver platter. You are striving to kill the white goose that laid the golden egg of civilization. If you succeed, you will not be able to get more golden eggs because the white goose will be dead.

They know that their race is a lower form of humanity and cannot stand on its own feet. The Africans of America are afraid to be without the white man, and thus, admit their own inferiority. Inferiors always demand the right to associate with their superiors. When the black man cries against segregation, he is actually singing praises to the white race.

AMERICA WAS FOUNDED BY WHITE MEN FOR WHITE MEN

They never intended for America to fall into the possession of a dark race. Many of the founders of this nation owned blacks as slaves, such as Washington, Jefferson, and the great Patrick Henry who said: "Give me liberty or give me death."

America is a white Christian nation and no infidelic religion such as **Islam has a** right to exist under the American sun. **Your Islam, your Mohammedanism is** not a white religion. Mohammedanism is a nigger religion. The white race will never accept it, so take it back to Africa with you. It is like the Holy **Bible** says about GOD'S plan for the nations of men in Acts 16:31 – "And hath determined the times before appointed, and the bounds of their habitation." Therefore you have no place in America with your African race or your Islamic African religion.

The Christian Party becomes stronger every day. When we are elected to power we will legally drive you out. Remember 1492 A.D. when those two great white Christian monarchs, King Ferdinand and Queen Isabella, expelled the Muslims from Spain. The Christian Party will be even more ruthless. We will not tolerate your infidelic Christ-hating religion on American soil. We will drive Islam into the ocean. America isn't big enough for the Christian Party and Black Islam, so Islam must go.

May God have mercy upon your heathen souls.

With many wishes for the failure of Islam in America, I am, Yours for Christ, Country and Race, (signed)

J.B. Stoner Archleader of the Christian Party

The following is the reply to Mr. Stoner's letter, sent to him a few days later by Elijah Muhammad.

THE SO-CALLED NEGROES' LOVE FOR WHITES:

The only so-called Negroes who love you (the whites) and desire you are those who are ignorant of the knowledge of you (this you do not know). And as soon as they awaken, as they will, to the knowledge of you being the real devils (their open enemies), they too will not shake your hands, nor want to look at you or even your shadow. The Truth of you will make all black mankind hate you, regardless of their color – black, brown, yellow or red. This Truth of you is part of that secret **that was withheld by** Allah, to allow you to live your Time (6000 years). (I admit that the so-called Negroes are not only ignorant of self and you but they are actually mentally dead). Your time is up and you are now being revealed, and you will by no means be able to hide yourself or deceive my people any longer.

THE MIXING OF BLACK AND WHITE BLOOD:

Who is to blame for this mixing – black Africans or the white European devils? **Did the black Africans go** seeking your white women in Europe or did you carry her to them in Africa? Isn't it true that **black Africans** are today asking your kind to leave them and their country, and that you won't leave without war? (They will one day throw you out!)

How did the so-called Negroes get into America? Did they come here of their own desire for America and for your women, or did YOU go after them in their country and bring them here against their will?

PROTECTION OF WOMEN:

Your concern for the protection of your white women should have been prepared by your fathers, and self, by staying away from our women. YOUR race is still white, so what are you afraid of?

You said we are 'Christ-hating'. You have used the name of Jesus for a bait to deceive the Negroes, while at the same time you are not a doer of the teachings of Jesus, nor of the Prophets before Jesus.

Your Bible teaches against the doing of evil. It also warns you to do unto others as you would have done unto yourself, and to love thy brother as thyself. Not any of these teachings have you or your kind ever practiced. You do not care enough for a Negro Christian believer to call him your brother Christian. And you do not think of doing unto him as you would have done unto yourself. You beat and kill them (Negro Christian believers) day and night and bomb their churches, where in reality they worship YOU, not Jesus. You even burn your own Christian

117

Sign (the Cross) when you plan to kill or burn your poor black Christian slaves.

Your Bible teaches that the 'Day' will come when every man will turn and go to his own. Did YOU originally own this part of our Planet? Aren't the red Indians the original owners, who are brothers of the dark Nation (of Islam) there is no part of our Planet that was ever given to the white race. The Planet belongs to US – the Nation of Islam! And I am afraid that you might fall backwards into a lake of fire when you attempt to drive **Islam** into the ocean. If the Ocean is ours, so is the land that you claim to be yours. Your Bible teaches you that it belongs to us. You shall soon come to know.

Your letter is headed with 1 **Thessalonians** 3:14-16 and St. John 8:44-48. Why not 2 **Thessalonians** 2:3, 4, 7-12; also 1 Corinthians 10:21. All these as well as St. John 8:44 refer to you and your race as the real devils, who even killed Jesus and the Prophets before Him, and who persecute us who believe and preach go to hell with you for believing and following you and your own Bible to pick that which condemns your own self!

(Signed: Elijah Muhammad)

Under the tutelage of Elijah Muhammad, the second "High Priest of the Black Race," Negroes took up the worship of the black race. As the leader of the largest black contingency of race worshipers in America, Elijah Muhammad found himself in the eye of a storm. The lynching, rape, and murder of Negroes were a common occurrence.

Throughout the south the most blatant forms of race worship imaginable were being put on public display for the whole world to see. Money, cars, homes, art, music, theaters, churches, books, newspapers, magazines, road signs, depots, restaurants, restrooms, water fountains, buses, trains, schools, universities, and even nooses were used to worship the white race. Worshipers were engulfed in total ecstasy, none more so than the members of the KKK who lived exclusively for the pleasure of the white race.

To appease the idol of the white race, the Klan performed rituals during which a cross was torched to boldly declare white supremacy. Any Negroes within sight of the cross were in danger of losing their lives. After being intoxicated by the brew of self-adulation cooked up during the ritual, Klan members took up arms and brazenly invaded Negro space. Their mission: terrorize the black population.

By law they could not take back control of Negro space but there was no law that prevented them from terrorizing it. Arsons, lootings, and lynchings were used as the instruments of terror. The Negroes may have space they control but they will never live in that space peaceably. These were the sentiments driving those who belonged to the Klan.

The siege continued for almost a century. Thousands of lives were lost and the damage to property was in the millions. The carnage sparked the great "Negro Migration" to the north. Fleeing the violence in the south, the Negro migrated north but encountered some of the same opposition. It appeared that everywhere the Negro settled his space came under siege.

Responding to the "Outcries for Justice," a great man in the personage of Dr. Martin Luther King, Jr. stood up in protest. At the time, Elijah was the reining "High Priest." Elijah took issue with Dr. King because he would not preach black separatism. A dispute erupted over what was the best way to live for the race. King wanted blacks and whites to live together in peace. He worked with whites and was not a Muslim sympathizer.

Elijah took issue with King's approach. He had this to say to Dr. King when they met in 1966: "Brother, you know a lot, but you don't understand very much." There is no record of anything Elijah said publicly in praise of Dr. King. On another occasion, Dr. King had this to say about Elijah after the two had dinner together: "I find no fault in the Honorable Elijah Muhammad."

King was a street fighter. He took the battle for equal rights to the streets. In doing so, he upstaged Elijah who fought his battles behind closed doors. Dr. King, in contrast, was a courageous man. He led from the front not from behind. From the podium and from the street, this fiery orator led a withering assault on white space. Assisted by then president Lyndon Baines Johnson, the walls protecting white space came tumbling down.

King not only fought to secure Negro space, he fought to make white space accessible. He gave his life so that Negroes could live in black or white space freely, if they chose. After the King insurrection, all that remained of the space that Jefferson allocated to whites was the "White space in the Mind."

King's sacrifice was total; he not only died for black people, he gave his life for all people. He was not a divisive force as he was accused of being. Dr. Martin Luther King, Jr. was a unifier. In the annals of American history, his achievements are unmatched. Since his death, Negro space has never been invaded. Those who reside there are free to live for the pleasure of the race.

End Notes
Chapter Six

[1] J. W. Randolph, "Notes on the State of Virginia," *Thomas Jefferson*, (1853).

7

Living for the Race

Life in America

Living for the race is the American way of life. In America everyone is confined to racial space and everything they do is a reflection of the race. To create this space, Jefferson and his cohorts got their hands dirty. They were intimately involved in the kidnapping, enslavement, maiming, torturing, raping, and killing of the people that laid the foundation for white space. It was they who established the tradition of racial domination that has continued up to the present day.

Those who live in white space owe the Founding Fathers a great debt of gratitude. The Founders made it possible for people today to enjoy racial domination and not be identified as racists. To show their appreciation, they have preserved the legacy of racial domination that the Founders put in place. Living for the white race means living above the black race. The best way to do this is to ensure that conditions in black space are deplorable.

Since blacks took control of black space some forty years ago conditions have greatly improved. The residents today include Supreme Court justices, secretaries of state, national security advisers, cabinet members, Senators, Congressmen, candidates for President, CEOs of major corporations, movie stars, entertainment moguls, pop icons, athletes, and a per capita income that surpasses most third world countries. Fancy cars, fancy homes, fancy clothes, fancy jobs and fancy education, it's hard to believe that less than two centuries ago most of the inhabitants of black space were slaves. Today it appears that everything is fine in black space. Appearances, however, can be deceiving. We realize this when we look at what is going on behind the façade.

In 2004 there were an estimated 400,000 children born to African American mothers. In the same year there were some 160,000 abortions. Of the 400,000 children that survived the womb, seventy percent were born out of wedlock; and of this seventy percent, thirty-five percent could not identify their biological father. African Americans, the latest incarnation of the Negro, have some of the highest rates of HIV infection, incarceration, single parenthood, obesity, high school dropouts, and divorce in America. Black on black crime, suicide, alcohol and drug abuse, moral decadence, and apathy are running rampant on the black reservation.

Arranging the external environment to reflect some fanciful notion of equality has failed to rid Negro space of the spirit of oppression. History seems to suggest that as long as Negro space is occupied, the spirit of oppression will reside there. It is visible in the hearts and minds of the people but it is not being properly identified. White oppression is easy to identify. When it occurs, the media is all over it. But when it is black oppression, blacks oppressing blacks, the incident is cleverly misrepresented. From the media perspective, blacks cannot oppress blacks; only whites can oppress blacks. When whites do it, it is more heinous because it crosses racial lines. This line of thinking is deceptive; it provides cover for the black oppressor. To get free from oppression, you must identify the oppressor. It's more difficult to identify the oppressor when he looks like you.

Those who have the greatest tendency to oppress are those who have been victims of oppression. Since its inception, Negro space has served as the seat of subjugation; the spirit of oppression dwells there with impunity. Captives in this space are conditioned to become oppressors.

The first oppressors were the white elite who prepared the space for the Negro. They controlled the space for almost two centuries and were forced to give it up after waging a fierce battle. The spirit of oppression never left the space. It entered the hearts and minds of Negroes who used its power to oppress one another.

Black Oppression

As oppressors, Negroes have done more to oppress their own people than any other people on earth. Not only do Negroes oppress one another, some act in ways that impede their own personal development. Those imbued with the rash of self-hatred willfully engage in acts of self-oppression. They hold themselves down and blame other people for their failure. Their greatest sense of accomplishment comes from bringing others down.

Who are these black oppressors? Some take roles as pimps, punks, thugs, hustlers, dealers, and players. Others take roles as criminals, absent fathers, unwed mothers, crooked politicians, greedy businessmen, and phony religionists. The number of roles is staggering, but the one thing they all have in common is that in their hearts the spirit of oppression is raging. As long as there is Negro space to occupy, they will always command a presence. The struggle to overthrow them will never end.

There are two camps of oppressors on the black reservation. One camp has positioned itself on the bottom rungs of society. From that position they pull everything down to them. Down is the direction they want to take society. These lowlifes are arrogant, condescending, shameless, irresponsible, disrespectful, loud, flashy, and uncouth. Their mission is the total degradation of mankind. Their tools are seduction, immorality, sexual perversion, violence, intimidation, deception, and vulgarity. They get paid for promoting their culture of sleaze.

The media has always had an affinity for degenerates. Glorifying reprobates has proven to be a very lucrative enterprise. They are rewarded for showing the public what the public wants to see. The public wants to see someone who looks like them. It doesn't matter if those who look like them are bottom feeders in the sewer.

In the other camp you find a different profile. In this camp are highly educated, well funded, clean cut, articulate professionals. This camp has positioned itself on top, and from that position they push everything downward. Their mission is to live above the fray. To remain above the fray they limit their contact with the great unwashed. Their main objective is to keep the riffraff beneath them. These polished Negroes comprise about ten percent of the black population. They engage in the more subtle form of oppression known as snobbery.

These snobs hold prominent positions on the black reservation. Puffed up by false pride they assume the position of the gatekeeper. The gatekeeper's job is to keep people on the reservation, behind the walls of the race. As gatekeepers they protect the interest of those who put them on top at the bottom. Gatekeepers knowingly and unknowingly are minions, stooges for white elite. White interest has not changed. What it is today is what it has always been about—racial domination. Anyone who is willing to support this effort on top or at the bottom of black society can get paid.

The spirit of oppression is fueled by greed. The typical payoff for the black oppressor at the top is tenure at a major white institution. To get tenure these oppressors surrender their hearts, minds, and souls to white ideals. For doing so they receive a nice salary, access to grant money, and the prestigious title of Ph.D. Very few actually live on the black reservation. Most live on the white reservation with the people that control them.

To maintain dominance, whites rely on black oppressors. These black oppressors will never admit that they are oppressors. It's not something that they do consciously. If you approach them and point out their complicity they will always deny it. The black oppressors are so self-absorbed that they don't even know they are oppressive. In their minds, enjoying life at someone else's expense has nothing to do with oppression. You owe them that because you're black. For that reason black oppression will never end. You cannot stop something you refuse to identify, especially when your excuse for doing so is that you're black.

"My race made me do that." Your race does not make you do anything. Race is just a shield you hide behind to avoid being held accountable. Race has been used to justify everything imaginable, including murder. And no one uses race as an excuse more than the black oppressor. Whatever I do to better myself, even if it's at your expense, is justified because we're both black. What a black man does to another black man or woman is between them, whites have nothing to do with it. If whites are not involved, it cannot be identified as oppression.

The unwillingness to identify and overthrow the oppressor makes the pressure created by those pushing down from the top and those pulling down from the bottom almost unbearable. To get relief, the people must overthrow these oppressors. What makes it so difficult is the fact that the oppressor looks like them.

Even if they could be overthrown, the sad truth is it would not change the position of black space. Regardless of who is in control, black space will always be at the bottom. The white oppressor will always see to that. White oppression, like black oppression, will never go away. It cannot go away because oppression is required to maintain white identity. Being white is about maintaining the top position. To do that the Negro must be kept at the bottom.

In order to claim whiteness you must first dismiss

blackness to some degree. Under no circumstances can whites allow Negroes to ascend to their level. If they do, being white loses it meaning. Whites must always remain vigilant in this regard. After all, the legacy of the Founding Fathers must be upheld. That legacy is one of racial domination. When being compared to Negroes, whites must always be conscious of whom and where they are, mentally and physically, at all times. There is nothing more demeaning for whites than to have a Negro above them. These were the heartfelt sentiments of Thomas Jefferson.

What would Jefferson think if he were here today? Would he be pleased with the current state of affairs? I don't think so. The system he masterminded and put into place is still functioning, but it by no means resembles what he originally established. If he were here today, I fear that he would curse the nation that he founded.

Maintaining the Space

Using the census, Jefferson created mental and physical space for the white race. That space was kept pure in his lifetime. No black could compete, especially in the arena of "white mind space." This mental space, once controlled exclusively by whites, has also given ground. There are whites today that readily admit that there are Negroes who are just as intelligent as they are. During Jefferson's time this was unheard of. After centuries of suppression, the intellect of those who represent the black race is finally being cultivated. This cultivation is taking place at the highest levels in society. It is even going on at the university Jefferson founded—the University of Virginia.

The same can be said about his old Alma Mater, the College of William and Mary.

The "white land space" that Jefferson reserved for whites has also taken a hit. The Negro invasion of white lands led by Martin Luther King, Jr. could not be repelled. The nightmare of Negroes owning and occupying white lands has become a reality. Jefferson's famous prediction that "blacks and whites cannot coexist without annihilating one another" has proven to be untrue.

Although tremendous change has occurred, the two spaces have remained intact. There has been no mass exodus from the white or black space. The current leaders have not allowed that to happen. Black space has three leaders: Louis Farrakhan who replaced Elijah Muhammad, and Jesse Jackson and Al Sharpton who replaced Dr. King.

Farrakhan, Jackson, and Sharpton are eminently qualified to hold their positions. They are avid race mongers who eat, sleep, and breathe race. For doing so, they are paid handsomely. At one time no one was paid to represent the black race. Today people earn millions. Race advocacy has become a very lucrative enterprise. These self-appointed "Race Lords" pride themselves on their ability to hold the white oppressor at bay while at the same time ignoring the transgressions of the black oppressor.

Using their twisted logic, black oppression must be excused by other blacks because it's being practiced by one of their own kind. If a black man is going to be strangled it's better to have black hands strangle him. Black hands violate him less than white hands. The black oppressor does not act out of hatred; the black oppressor is driven by hopelessness. There is a difference. The greater outrages, of course, are the atrocities committed by whites.

Loathing the Leader of the White Race

There are those who believe that the white race does not have leaders. Unlike Jessie Jackson and Al Sharpton, no one has come forward to publicly declare that he or she is the leader of the white race. This does not mean that the white race does not have leaders. The white race has leaders and the leaders make the dictates of the white race known on a daily basis. They make them known the way they have always made them known—through the media.

The use of the term African American was not decided by the people the term identifies. There was no petition circulated to determine if the term African American was acceptable. The people had no say in the matter; the decision was made by the media. The media has always had the power to impose the dictates of the white race on the black minority. When the media grows tired of the term African American a new term will be interjected and the black minority will roll over once again and accept it

The dictates of the race have always been communicated by the media. In the early days, the media comprised newspapers, magazines, books, and journals. Using these vehicles, the race made its dictates known. Today, in the age of advanced communications, the race uses political commentators to get the word out. One such commentator is Rush Limbaugh, the current "High Priest of the White Race."

Limbaugh performs his duties as a spokesman for the white race behind his "Golden EIB Microphone." On his radio talk show, Limbaugh, the most dangerous man in America, ties half his brain behind his back just to make it fair. Sitting in his famous "Attila the Hun Chair," Limbaugh, who describes himself as a harmless little fuzz ball, goes about the business of keeping the Jefferson legacy of racial domination alive.

The fact that Jefferson was an avowed white supremacist does not seem to bother Ol' Rush. After all, where would America be without racial domination? The American economy, if my memory serves me correctly, was jumpstarted by the subjugation of people Jefferson referred to as the inferior race.

Billions of dollars are spent each year producing, advertising, and packaging products that appeal to a particular race. To promote their race, people in America pay millions. No one does a better job promoting the white race and is rewarded more handsomely for doing so than Rush Limbaugh. Jackson, Sharpton and Farrakhan combined will not receive $400 million over the next eight years. So why is a man being paid this sum of money to represent the white race complaining about someone representing the black race? Is it possible that the most intelligent man in America does realize that he is in the race business?

What Limbaugh does, he does brilliantly. On a daily basis, he gives marching orders to millions of people. At his "Institute for Advanced Conservative Studies," he teaches his students that conservatism rather than liberalism is the best way to live for the white race. Living as a conservative, Limbaugh illustrates how racial domination can be imposed without offending the "black guy." Using economics, he teaches his students that the best way to keep blacks in their places is to outspend them. This can be done in a congenial way without provoking animosity.

Increased consumption is Limbaugh's answer for everything. Following this line of thinking, all whites have to do to maintain Jefferson's legacy of racial domination is to increase their consumption. Increasing consumption is not very difficult for those who are the prime beneficiaries of racial privilege.

In order for one group to enjoy racial privilege, another group must be denied. If no one were favored it would not be a privilege. The identity of the people who enjoy favor has never changed; they created the system. The favor being sought has always been economic. To avail themselves of favor, all they have to do is give a face to the race, a white face.

White privilege is about access to capital. In America, access to capital has always been controlled by men with white faces. When you control access to capital you control the markets. To bring a product to market you must have capital. To access capital you must approach those who control it. The people who have the best access to capital are those who are favored by racial privilege. Decisions based on race that grant access to capital have corrupted the culture of capitalism. Even without this corruption the culture is critically flawed.

The flaw lies in its basic premise that individual greed is virtuous. The lifeblood of capitalism is greed, the desire to possess more than you actually need. To satisfy this desire you must consume. Your capability to consume determines your status in a capitalistic society. The more you consume, the more you become attached. The propensity to become attached is unlimited.

Through the marvels of mass media, consumers become attached to things that only exist on the drawing board. Our penchant to consume things is only surpassed by our attachment to them. Attachment occurs because capitalism at its core is about exhibitionism. Those who consume more put on the best shows, as Limbaugh illustrates.

No one should object to this passive form of white oppression, not even blacks. After all, according to Limbaugh everyone benefits from a vibrant economy. Passive oppression, the new genre being practiced by "Maha Rushie" and his ilk is no different than the blatant oppression being espoused by David Duke. The two are one and the same because the objective is to maintain racial domination. The minor difference is that those who practice passive oppression are not pegged to racism. To provide themselves cover, these passive oppressors place blacks around the periphery of their inner circle. These high-tech Uncle Toms act as protective shields that provide the oppressors deniability. They do so in the guise of so-called black conservatism. If conservatism is so great, why are distinctions made according to race? Why are you white or black before you are conservative?

The black conservatives pride themselves for being on top at the bottom. They share space on top at the bottom with black liberals. Both are creations of the white power structure on both sides of the political spectrum. The division on top at the bottom has created a power struggle between black conservatives and black liberals. This skirmish provides another layer of insulation for the white establishment.

The same skirmish, however, is going on in the white race on top at the top. Although there may appear to be unity, there has never been a unified white race. The quest for racial domination came closer to unifying the white race than any other endeavor but there was always dissension in the ranks. That dissension led to the abolishment of slavery.

Dissension will never go away. Today we find it in the split between white liberals and white conservatives. The animosity between the two camps is palpable, which makes it more difficult to maintain the status quo.

The integrity of racial space cannot be maintained without some form of oppression. The spirit of oppression is tied to race. Neither party wants to take action that would be interpreted as oppressive and risk being accused of being a racist. Racial sensitivity today is at an all time high, which makes this an ideal time to resolve the race issue.

To resolve the issue, both parties, the oppressors and the oppressed, the liberal and the conservative, must abandon race. To be liberated, the people on the black and white reservation must put down the brooch of racial identity and leave the reservation. Unfortunately there is no liberal or conservative proposal to put an end to race. This is perhaps the greatest challenge Americans could ever undertake. The challenge is far more difficult for whites than it is for blacks because whites have more to lose. Anyone who puts down a white brooch will loose his or her position on top.

The white reservation in America is the most sought after place on earth. Millions of people all over the world have been waiting in line for years to get in. Some even risk their lives crossing the border illegally so that they might live on the white reservation. Everyone wants to be on top, no one wants to live at the bottom. People at the bottom in their homeland come to America so that they can live on top. No one comes to America to live at the bottom, not even Africans. This does not mean, however, that there are no people living at the bottom. If there were no people at the bottom there would no people on top.

Most people know before they arrive that the Negro is at the bottom. They also know that to enjoy the top position they must keep the Negro in his place. Otherwise they too may end up at the bottom.

In a capitalistic society, being on top is everything. Because it's everything, the Negro cannot rely on whites and their surrogates to resolve the race issue. Neither can the Negro rely on black leaders who engage them in race worship. Race worship has value only for those who are seeking racial domination. It is of no value to those who want to be liberated from race.

Taught in the black church, black liberation theology is a great case in point. Those who practice this theology believe that to achieve liberation the people must approach God cloaked in the garb of the race. Being worshiped by the race, God will be moved to act favorably upon them. From where have these teachings come? No one has been authorized to approach God on behalf of the black race. The black race has never chosen anyone to represent its interest before God. The people who have taken these positions have done so of their own volition and without a clear understanding of what race is.

There is only one race. Anyone who approaches God on behalf of the black race has been deceived. Race is man's invention. It was created to impose domination. For race to stand, one race must dominate another race. Why would you approach God in the name of the black race if you are not prepared to dominate the white race?

Representing the black or the white race is a captive state. It doesn't matter if you are bound up on top or bound up at the bottom; you are still bound up. As long as you are living for the race you will never know liberation.

Setting the Stage

By unleashing the forces of lust, greed, anger, false pride, hatred, envy, and egotism, with race as a backdrop, America engaged in the most massive *external undertaking* in the history of mankind. For all intents and purposes, American civilization can be summed up in two words, "racial theatrics."

The original writers, actors, producers, and directors of this theatrical gem were none other than the Founding Fathers. Cast in the roles of whites, blacks, and Indians, Americans were engaged in a dramatic portrayal depicting external life. The performers on this magnificent stage were chosen for their roles based solely on their external attributes.

The first role filled was that of the white male. The Founding Fathers themselves were the first to assume this role. To qualify, all they had to do was to show up white, male, and be staunch advocates for the white race. Because this was the starring role, the Founders were eager to perform. Those who performed admirably were guaranteed a page in the historical record. In the role of the white male, they were the closest things to God on earth. The American white male decided who lived and who died, who was enslaved and who was free. No one was above him. He had the final say in all of the affairs of state. He could lie, cheat, steal, rape, murder, and oppress, and never fear retribution. There was nothing that he could not do in the role of the white male.

The second role assigned was that of the white female. This role demanded purity, grace, dedication, and submissiveness. The women who assumed this role were powerful like their white male counterparts, but their power had limitations. There were certain things they could not do in the role of the white female; among them, vote and hold public office. This was in accordance with the law. The script, as it was originally written, placed limitations on the freedoms of the white female. The writers, producers, and directors were careful to protect the interest of the white male.

The third role assigned was that of the Indian or Native American. To fit the profile, the red man had to be meek, humble, and submissive, willing to succumb to the wishes of the white man. Native Americans did not fit the profile the Founders were looking for but could not be denied a role on the stage of external life. The role they chose to play was that of warriors. In this role they wreaked havoc, which could not be tolerated. To restore order, the Native Americans were removed from the stage of external life.

The fourth and final role assigned was that of the Negro. Those chosen to assume this role were abducted from Africa. Africans were black, strong, simplistic, and thought to be less intelligent, which fit the profile that the writers, directors, and producers were looking for. The first candidates, however, showed no interest in performing as representatives of the black race. They were not eager to be cast in the role of savage beasts that were less than human. Africans, unlike Native Americans, had been purchased. An investment had been made to acquire them. To banish them like Native Americans would not be cost effective. Instead of removing them from the stage, they were kept in the background.

After years of discord and reprisals which included sexual improprieties, the Founders, yielding to their lower nature, sired a number of imps with African women they raped. These imps were trained to become the first representatives of the black race. Born in captivity, they performed the role of the Negro to perfection.

Great theatrical performances require a grand stage. To construct this grand stage with its elaborate façades a new industry was brought into being. To construct the façades, an enormous labor pool was required that worked behind the scenes. The set of the plantation is where most of the early productions took place. The plantation was an ideal setting to showcase the four principle characters in this great American epic, "Living for the Race." The performers in the role of the white male were cast as presidents, senators, congressmen, governors, mayors, pastors, sheriffs, judges, lawyers, jurist, soldiers, planters, overseers, and slave owners. Those performing in the role of the white female were cast as the wives, mothers, grandmothers, sisters, daughters, and mistresses of the white male. To give balance to the epic, the black race was also represented. The performers chosen for this role were cast as male and female slaves.

The motive behind producing this grand spectacle was not to entertain an audience; the principle objective was commerce. Making money. Everyone associated with the production was paid except those in the role of the Negro. It was never the intention of the writers, directors, or producers to pay those who performed as Negroes. Even though their hands and backs served as the economic base on which the production rested, no one was paid to represent the black race. Only those who represented the white race were rewarded.

Putting together a theatrical performance of this magnitude was a costly affair. To offset the cost and turn a profit, the products and services provided by free labor were marketed. The free labor was provided by those who performed as Negroes. The plantation was an ideal setting for conducting such an enterprise. Those portraying the white male took great pleasure in performing on this magnificent stage. It was on this stage that some of the greatest performances in American history were turned in. Thomas Jefferson, James Monroe, and James Madison were three of the early greats. They performed superbly on the American stage of external life. Some of their most memorable performances took place on the set of the Southern plantation. Under the mesmerizing spell of racial grandeur these men were completely transformed. After undergoing transformation, they actually became the characters they were portraying. The writers, the directors, and the producers did an excellent job crafting these leading roles. It was made easier by the fact that the performers took great pride and were honored to perform in the role of the slave master.

As the writers, directors, producers, and actors, the Founding Fathers staged the greatest show on earth. Since premiering in the 1700s, this show has captivated the imagination of the entire world. Lured by the prospect of racial domination, people have come from every corner of the globe to see and take part in the great American epic, "Living for the Race." The modern performances still feature racial domination but are not nearly as grandiose as they once were. The current writers, directors, and producers have changed the set and the script. Some of the more diabolical roles such as the slave master and the slave have been omitted from the plot. Gone from the stage are the blood curdling scenes of performers being killed for their portrayal of Negroes. Nothing gave the performance a greater sense of realism than the actual killing of the performers. Until the great American epic "Living for the Race" premiered, there was no show staged that featured the killing of the performers.

Today, things have changed. Not only are those who represent the black race paid, they are paid handsomely. The term used to identify them has also changed—from Negro to African American. On occasion there are scenes where a performer representing the black race is killed by representatives of the white race but the perpetrators no longer go unpunished.

Those who perform as whites no longer get away with murder as they once did. The license to kill for the race has expired. The plot has been rewritten, due in part to the demand for better roles by those who represent the black race. Unlike the early days there are now limits on what a performer can do as a representative of the white race.

Standing in Defiance

In the final analysis, there is no white or black race; only people conditioned to perform racial roles. The conditioning that goes on is an imposition. Because it begins at an early age, there is little or no resistance. How can a child resist? The question, "Why should I live for the race?" is never debated. The body, mind, and spirit are surrendered without deliberation. Because there is no discussion most people cannot remember making the transition to race. They falsely claim that they have always lived for the race.

When you live for the race, to preserve your identity you must impose race on others. Viewing others racially is an imposition. Not everyone lives for the race. When this is pointed out, most people are perplexed because they view everyone racially. They find it difficult to understand why anyone would not identify with their race.

On the stage of external life, everyone identifies with race. Living for the race is one of America's oldest pastimes, but not all Americans participate. This has been the case since the nation was founded. Even though the branch of the race was extended to all newcomers, not everyone accepted. There were those who chose to live beyond the race. Although most had white skin, they did not represent the interest of the white race. The same was true for those with dark skin. These people did not please the race; they found their solace in doing what was right. It was their valiant effort that freed the slaves. John Brown and the Grimké sisters, Sarah and Angelina were among them.

John Brown   *Angelina Grimké*   *Sarah Grimké*

Because they stood in opposition to the interest of the white race, they were viewed as traitors and turncoats. Their activities were undertaken to undermine the very institution on which white domination was built. Assisted by others with a similar mindset, their dream of abolishing slavery was realized. For their efforts there were little or no thanks. Not even from the people they set free. Their contribution to American society in terms of restoring civility is monumental but their accomplishments have never been properly recognized. The people who benefited most from their heroic deeds have not found the character to show them fitting appreciation. There have been no efforts to establish holidays, streets, parks, or monuments in their memory.

Those who represent the black race have not been able to reconcile in their minds, actions taken by those who live beyond race. This is due in part to the inability they have to live beyond race. To preserve their identity, those who represent the black race must view everyone racially.

This being the case, the people who live beyond race are not visible. The only things visible are those things their racial template reveals, which are external.

8

The External Truth

Racial Liberation

The quest for racial liberation will never end. Racial space is constructed in such a way that someone has to be at the bottom. There are only two ways to seek liberation: one is total separation as was proposed by Marcus Garvey, and the other approach is to overthrow the current oppressors and become the dominator.

In an unofficial survey conducted at a public gathering, four hundred African Americans were asked the following question:

If the United States government decided to award three states, Alabama, Mississippi, and Louisiana, to African Americans as a form of reparations, would you choose to reside there?

144

Ninety percent of the respondents answered no. Forty-five percent refused to even consider living separately from whites. Based on the rate of black on black crime some African Americans believe that a black society could not survive without the presence of whites. Many believe that blacks are too soft on crime, and thus lack the conviction required to police the community. Based on these sentiments separation appears not to be an option.

The other approach is to overthrow the current oppressor. To accomplish this, the desire for black domination must be cultivated. Currently that desire does not exist. The oppressed are not clamoring to take the position of the oppressor. Based on how the space has been constructed, to be liberated blacks must take the position of dominance. In America whites have always dominated. Blacks have never enjoyed the dominant position.

Race was born from the quest for white domination. Until blacks have the numbers, the desire, and the resources to overthrow the white dominator, black liberation in America will never occur.

Even if by some fluke the blacks turned the tables and found themselves in the dominant position, would that eliminate the need for racial liberation? Changing the oppressor at the top is not going to end the struggle. In the space created by race there will never be peace. The quest for liberation will continue as long as there is someone at the bottom.

Would black domination be accepted by whites? Within the context of this question we see why the race issue cannot be resolved racially. The solution is not race; race is the conundrum and it becomes bigger each time the brooch of racial identity is taken up. To resolve the issue, race must be dismantled.

Who Is Really in Control?

There are two ways to approach human life: external and internal. Using the external approach you must lend yourself to the process of acquisition. The process begins in earnest when you attach yourself to race.

Attaching yourself to race puts you in a position where you are owed something. According to the Founding Fathers, if the race you attach yourself to is white you are owed racial privilege. You deserve the top position.

Those who feel they are owed something never show appreciation. The entitlement mentality will not permit it. They bask in the grandeur of conceit and false pride. For that reason they are denied the ability to love. What they come to know as love is lust.

There is no love on the stage of external life. Love cannot exist in this racially charged environment. Lusting is what you do when you attach yourself to external things to establish an identity. Race is external; attaching yourself to race is an act of lust. The connection is made to facilitate domination.

In America the people in the best position to dominate are those with white skin. On the stage of external life, no one has more access to resources than those who represent the white race. Although one may find comfort in being the dominator there is an unforeseen danger, the danger of becoming deluded.

Delusion sets in when the performers think that the props on the stage, the house they live in, the car they drive, and the role they are playing, actually belong to them. Because the role of dominator encompasses a lifetime, those who are deluded do not realize that nothing belongs to them. At the time of death, the house, the car, the money, and the race are taken from them. Perhaps only after everything has been lost do they realize that living for the race is theatrics.

On the stage of external life no one owns anything. The harsh reality is everything belongs to the government, including the race. What you claim to be your race has validity only if it is recognized by the state. Only under the auspices of the government, does the race have legal standing. Without the backing of the state, the race has no sovereignty.

In its infancy, racism in America was mandated and sanctioned by the government. As the government's chosen minion, race was used as a restraining device. To secure domination, rights were extended to the white race as a body but no term was used to identify the body. The term, "white race" does not appear anywhere in the founding documents. Because the body was not identified it was not subject to prosecution.

As an entity unto itself, the white race could not be held liable for any action taken on its behalf. Acting as agents of the race, government officials could engage in the lynching of blacks and not have the race or the government implicated. There were two institutions operating simultaneously but only one was identified. A concerted effort was made at least on paper to maintain the *"separation between race and state."*

The Declaration of Independence written by Thomas Jefferson did not contain language that referred to the white race. "We hold these truths to be self evident that all men are created equal, that they are endowed by their creator with certain unalienable rights, that among these are: life, liberty, and the pursuit of happiness," refers to citizens of the state. The race of the citizens is not mentioned. The power was vested in the state, not in the race.

The founding documents omitted any language that referred to the rights of the white race. Although the rights of the white race were not clearly delineated in the founding documents the implications were clear. What the Founders did not say in writing, they expressed through their actions. No action was taken by any of the signers that recognized the rights of blacks. To maintain the *"separation between race and state"* they spoke on behalf of the state but acted on behalf of the race.

Speaking on behalf of the state provided them cover, as was the case with Thomas Jefferson. As a man of the state, Jefferson spoke about freeing his slaves but as a man of the race he did nothing. In his lifetime he did not free one slave. Jefferson owned more than one hundred slaves and a number of them were unable to work because of their age. Freeing an old slave would have given Jefferson the statesman credibility but Jefferson the white male did not free slaves.

Although the rights of the white race were not put in writing they could be clearly understood by observing the actions of the Founders. The only thing left open to debate was what the limitations were. Where did the rights of the white race end and the rights of the black race begin? Based on the actions of the Founders, blacks had no rights.

The Bill of Rights did not pertain to blacks. In fact there were no rights extended to blacks by any of the founding documents. From this one might conclude that the government was acting on behalf of the white race.

Although action could be taken on behalf of the race, the race as a body had no legislative or judicial power ceded to it by the Constitution. The *"separation between race and state"* was maintained to ensure that the government did not have to answer to any claim made against the white race.

Any liability for action taken on behalf of the race falls squarely in the lap of the individual. There is nothing that legally binds the government to race. Even though this massive theatrical performance is owned and operated by Uncle Sam, the government also has the power to shut it down. With a stroke of the pen the government can shut down race in America. This could be done by removing the category of race from the census.

Governments exist to govern. To govern, people and space are required. At no time does the government relinquish its sovereignty over its people or its space. Everyone must pay income and property taxes and is subject to eminent domain. The government reserves the right to regulate what you do as an individual on the property you occupy. It only allows the user and the space to be used in accordance to dictates that are prescribed by law. These laws are designed to enhance the quality of life of the individual and to increase the overall livability of the space.

To implement its dictates, the mechanism chosen by the American government is race. Race is the restraining device that the government uses to control the interactions of its citizenry. Prior to America's founding, the governments of other nations used the royal family and religion to implement their dictates. American was the first nation on earth to use race as a regulatory device.

Using the apparatus we know as the census, the government allocates identity and space to its populace. As a tool, the census is as powerful today as it was when James Madison introduced it. The government is empowered by the census to provide the incentive people need to live for the race. But by making one simple change that power can be rendered mute. The census derives its power from using the term race, removing the category of race would eliminate government dependency.

Of course, this may never happen because the government relies on race to create dependency. The people who depend most on race are those who receive government handouts. They would not receive these handouts if it were not for race.

The competition between the races is the fuel that drives the juggernaut of American Civilization. Race has proven itself to be one of the best motivators known to man. It built the greatest empire in the history of mankind. Race built America. American culture is race. Without race there would be no America.

The empire that race built, however, is external and because it's external its operation is inefficient. To advance it must rely on depreciation. Someone's life is assigned less value because of race. As a result of being marginalized, these lives rarely develop to their full potential. The loss of human potential that has occurred since this practice was adopted is staggering.

Race is driven by dissension; one group is pitted against another. For government, dissension among the races is a boon. It keeps attention focused on the stage, not on what's going on behind the scenes. On the stage the people are engaged in external life, which maintains their external connection.

The Forest of External Life

The stage of external life is analogous to a forest. For those who live in this forest, success is determined by how well you decorate your tree. Nice house, nice job, nice bank account, nice car, nice neighborhood, nice boat, nice friends, nice computers, nice pets, nice swimming pool, everything placed on the tree has to be nice. Success is an image. To create the image the ornaments on the tree are valued more than the tree they decorate.

In the forest of external life there are white trees, red trees, yellow trees, and black trees. These trees are manmade and they belong to the race. Of all the trees in the forest, the trees that are admired most are white. The white trees have the nicest decorations. This leads some to conclude that the white trees are healthier and therefore superior.

The health of a tree is determined by the condition of its roots. To examine the roots you must look beyond the nice decorations. The roots of the tree are not visible. To examine the root you must do some digging. Digging in the forest of external life you find that none of the trees have roots. In this forest dead trees are being decorated. What difference does it make if the white trees have nicer decorations? Decorating a dead tree is an act of futility. Those engaged in this process squander precious human life. They take pleasure in having a dead tree admired.

These trees belong to the race and are decorated for the race. The cost of decorations is what drives the American economy. When you live for the race, even though you purchased it, the image that you see in the mirror does not belong to you even though it may have cost you thousands of dollars. Nothing belongs to you, not your family, your culture, your faith, or even your God. To live for the race you must give everything to the service of the race: what you wear, what you eat, how you speak, what you think, how you act, and what you create.

To represent the race you must surrender everything, and for doing so you are given no voice in determining what course or objective the race pursues. You belong to something that you cannot regulate. Living for the race is not living for yourself. It's a life you live according to the dictates of others. When you live for others, you have no control. The identity and the space you occupy are created for you, not by you. Instead of defining yourself, you are being defined.

Fear and Anxiety

The assimilation of race trips the release mechanism that puts the wheel of external life into motion. Once in motion everything is viewed externally, which distorts human perception. Viewing humanity through the prism of race fosters division. This division generates anxiety, which manifest as fear, envy, mistrust, bigotry, and hatred. As long as race is allowed to stand, this anxiety will never be alleviated. The anxiety is generated by the fear of loss. For race to stand, one race must dominate another. You cannot have race without a top and bottom. Because those on top have the power, they have the greater fear of loss.

The sense of identity that we first develop is one of proprietorship. We know ourselves first as proprietors.

To become a proprietor, you must attach yourself to something. What you attach yourself to, such as, your name, your gender, your race, your relationships, and your possessions, forms your identity.

In the realm of externals, your frontline identity, what you identify with first, is the element that allows you to claim the most assets. In America the identity that gives you the most clout is being a white male or female. Being white allows Bobby and Sue to connect to the Founding Fathers. Being black only allows Billy and Julie to connect to the slaves of the Founders. From this historic perspective, you see why white identity has always been on top and black identity has always been at the bottom.

In America space was constructed for whites on top and blacks at the bottom. This space is still being occupied today. Although conditions have changed on the top and at the bottom, two things remain the same—fear and anxiety. Fear and anxiety will never go away because living for the race imposes isolation.

Living in a Bubble

To live for the race you must adopt behavior that preserves your racial identity. One such behavior is to place yourself inside a racial bubble. To preserve white identity space is sequestered by those with white skin. Space is also sequestered by those with dark skin. This space imposes isolation.

Race in its most subtle form is negative space. The space is created to impose domination and is divided into quadrants. The white quadrant is on top, the black quadrant is at the bottom, and the other two quadrants are in between. No people have had less control of the space they occupy than those in the black quadrant. The first occupants of this space were held captive in shackles and chains.

Each quadrant contains bubbles. The individuals in the quadrants occupy space inside these bubbles. To maintain the sanctity of the space inside the bubble, it can only be shared with those who have similar bubbles. Allowing someone in a black bubble to enter space inside a white bubble is viewed as a breech. For those who allow their bubbles to be breeched, there are serious consequences, among them excommunication.

In the negative space that race creates there are two dynamics at play. One force imposes racial domination, while the other force opposes it. In racial space, race puts you on top or it puts you at the bottom. After a fierce struggle, those at the bottom have taken control of the space they occupy. In some minds this is viewed as a great accomplishment. What they fail to see is that controlling the space at the bottom keeps them at the bottom.

The conditions on the bottom have changed but the position is still the same. The nature of race is such that nothing you do at the bottom can change the position of the space. The people at the bottom will always be looking up. The only recourse is to leave the space they rely on for identity. Sharing space at the bottom gave life to black identity, just as sharing space on top gave life to white. New space must be created that will give life to a new identity.

The power vested in the top position is the impetus that created white space. Those who taste the bitter potion of racial domination never give it up. Drunk on the power of ascendancy they unwittingly submit to life inside a white bubble.

Imposing domination or resisting domination are both captive states. To pursue either one you must live inside a bubble. Are those trapped on top really better off than those trapped at the bottom? Externally it may appear so, but when viewed internally they are both the same.

Bondage is bondage. What difference does it make if you are bound up in golden chains or iron? The power to dominate is not the greater power. The greater power is the power to liberate. Everyone cannot become a dominator, but everyone can become a liberator. Liberating is much easier than dominating; all you have to do is burst the racial bubble.

To enjoy domination, isolation is the price that you must pay. The negative space that race creates cannot be maintained without isolation. Racial isolation created the top and bottom positions. Maintaining the sanctity of the space is the first priority. On top, the space is valued more than the race. Race is of little consequence if you fail to maintain the sanctity of the space. To maintain its sanctity it must be restricted. You can only share the space with someone who looks like you. You did not create the space. The space was created for you by the Founders. To please the Founders all you have to do as a white male or female is to maintain the sanctity of the space. To maintain its sanctity you must avail yourself of racial privilege. When something exclusive is offered that is unavailable to blacks, you must accept it. Few things do more to maintain the sanctity of white space than the offering and acceptance of white privilege. When privilege is rejected, the sanctity of white space is violated. To be proven worthy to occupy the space you must accept white privilege.

Other tests to prove your worthiness are those that force you to engage in blatant acts of racism. Nothing authenticates your worthiness more than showing your hatred for blacks. These acts run the gamut. They can be as simple as using the "N" word or as vicious as dragging someone to death behind a pickup truck. Everyone inside a white bubble has to undergo a worthy test. The same is true of those in black bubbles.

A great case in point is President Barak Obama. When Obama first appeared on the scene, the question was asked, "Is Obama's bubble black enough?" After intense scrutiny some now believe that Obama's bubble is too black. Like whites do to authenticate their whiteness, it appears that Obama, following that tradition, is now the recipient of black privilege in the form of the black vote.

The black vote authorizes him to represent black folks. Obama has also engaged in what some consider blatant acts of racism. To authenticate his blackness, Obama sat in a church for twenty years and heard the minister vilify the white race. In doing so, he passed the test. He proved that he is worthy, but what does that really mean?

For those in white bubbles, it means it's time to rally the troops. Obama's election marks the end of America's legacy of white domination. At no time in history has the legacy of the Founding Fathers suffered a greater blow, not even during the Civil War. Whiteness today faces its greatest challenge ever and everyone in a white bubble is going to be tested. At issue is: how to maintain racial domination?

For the Founders of this nation, nothing is more symbolic of white domination than having a white male in the White House. Allowing a black man to enter the White House to lead the nation they founded is the ultimate insult. If Thomas Jefferson were here today he would be outraged. Even if Obama was the most qualified man in America there is no way that Jefferson would support him, and those who preserve his legacy know this. Under no circumstances can this be allowed to stand and those who are guardians of the legacy will do everything in their power to ensure that President Obama fails.

At no time since the Civil War has the political climate in America been so explosive. The level of hatred between liberals and conservatives reached an all-time high during the Clinton years. No one contributed more to this volatile political climate than Rush Limbaugh. For eight years, Limbaugh pummeled Bill Clinton. The level of vitriol heaped on Clinton in the form of inflammatory rhetoric was unprecedented. It took the standards of political discourse down to an all-time low. The blowback in response by liberals was a vicious attack of a conservative in the person of George Bush. The liberal assault on Bush was the payback.

What can Obama expect? Clinton only had one strike against him—he was liberal. Obama has two—not only is he liberal, he's black. Will Limbaugh ratchet up the rhetoric so high that it inflames the racist elements of the conservative party?

What would happen to the country if President Obama were assassinated? Some fear that every major city in America would burn. Race relations in the country would be set back one hundred years. The fear of this happening was never discussed in the media during the election. What does this say about America today? Is America ready for President Obama? There are those who will go to any length to maintain the persona of racial dominance. For them no price is too high to pay.

Who Obama is, is less important than what he represents. Obama represents the end of racial domination. Racial domination built this country and for those residing in white bubbles maintaining this legacy is essential. For them, Obama's greatest threat is not that he lives for the pleasure of the black race; it's the power he has to burst the racial bubble. No one who has entered the White House has been in a better position to do so.

President Obama may not know that he has this power. As long as he is trapped inside a black bubble he cannot exercise it. To liberate others he must first liberate himself. To liberate himself he must burst his bubble.

For Obama, bursting the bubble would not be difficult; the only thing required is sound vibration. Sound created race and sound can destroy it. By uttering these words publicly, *"I am not your black President,"* Obama can burst his racial bubble. This sound vibration creates space beyond race. Creating this space is not difficult; the greater challenge is maintaining it. To maintain this space he must deal with the consequences of creating it.

Uttering these words, *"I am not your black President,"* Obama would upset those who reside in black bubbles. He earned his popularity by endearing himself to the race. For those who occupy black bubbles this is a pivotal moment. At no time in history has the space inside the bubble been more comforting and no one should be more comfortable than President Obama.

Uttering the words, *"I am not your black President,"* would destroy the space that allowed him to assume the most powerful position in the world. In this position he is the master, not the servant. He's the head, not the tail. He's the beginning, not the end. And no one has more power.

With this power, President Obama can shut down race in this country. A majority of the American people have put him in a position to do just that. His election is evidence that America is ready for change. The question is will he do it? If he did, would America follow his lead? If he were to burst his racial bubble, how would America respond?

The theme of the Obama campaign was change. Some have mistaken the change that he referred to, to mean change at the top. Nothing is going to change at the top; the political culture in America has always been corrupt and no one man can change it. The change that President Obama was speaking of was change at the bottom. The people at the bottom, the grassroots, have always had the power to change this nation. The evidence of that ability is the election of Obama. He has provided a catalyst for unity like America has never known.

The test of a true leader is not what he does for the people. The test of a true leader is what he inspires people to do for one another. The biggest obstacle in this regard has always been race.

The America that I Love

America is the greatest nation on earth. That greatness, however, has only been partially realized. To realize its fullness, America must turn inward. Using the same energy and ingenuity that built the world's greatest external empire, America can build the greatest internal empire. The two empires can exist together within the same structure.

To take up this challenge, the American lifestyle must be balanced. Until now, there has been no desire for balance. The American people have allowed race to dominate the culture. The election of President Obama is a signal for change. It is the most significant easing of racial suppression in the history of the nation. America is turning away from race. This movement away has to be viewed with great optimism. What would America be if the American people could live beyond race?

PART TWO

Living
Internal
life

9

Living Beyond Race

Our nature as human beings is such that we rely on attachments to sustain us. We attach ourselves to things that give us life. The attachments take place externally and internally. The first thing that we attach ourselves to is our mother. In the womb, the infant is connected to its mother by an umbilical cord. Having this external connection is critical; it provides needed nourishment without which the infant would not survive. After birth, an attachment develops internally. The infant attaches itself internally to the things that sustain life. The attachment develops in response to impulses that emanate from within. These impulses generate anxiety in the form of hunger, thirst, and fatigue. To mitigate this anxiety, the child seeks relief in the form of food, drink, and sleep. Quelling this anxiety awakens the first sense of self, which is perceived to be internal.

Responding to the anxiety within, we come to know ourselves initially as internal beings. The first segment of our lives is spent freeing the space within from anxiety. The first peace that we come to know as humans is freedom from hunger, thirst, and fatigue. Finding peace within fixes our perceptual reality. The first identity we project is from an internal place. We claim that place as our own.

The hunger, thirst, and fatigue that you experience belong to you. The depth of your attachment to food, drink, and sleep, determines how you deal with your anxiety. Responding to hunger, thirst, and fatigue is your responsibility. Only you know what's going on in your space. This changes however when you take the stage of external life. On this stage the space you claim expands. The expansion occurs when you assume your role. The role is the umbilical cord that connects you to the race. ***The race is the extended body. This body has no life of its own.*** To be given life it has to be connected, and the connection is made when the role is assumed—the role of living for the race.

When you assume the role, you claim the space that race occupies. Everyone is connected by the role. The role is the attachment that gives life to the body of the race. Race does not give you life; you give life to race. Giving life to race gave birth to America. America is the land of race. The American people live and die for the race. Under no circumstances would a true American question his race.

Why would you question the white race? Your race is on top, it's superior. You run the show. Nothing on earth is more powerful than the white race, so why would you question it?

No one questions race, not even those at the bottom. At one time the black race, like the white race, was non-existent. There were no people living for the race. The body of the race had no life. The race role was rejected. To give life to the black race someone had to assume the role at the bottom.

Knowing what the role implies, why would anyone assume the bottom position? This is a question that deserves an answer, but no one questions race. Instead they give life to race—by living it.

Giving Life to Race

For what purpose was race given life? The white race was the first to appear. It was given life to impose domination. To subjugate people with darker skin, physical, mental, and spiritual repression was employed. This action created the space that the races occupy.

Finding peace in external space is very difficult. It is far more difficult than finding peace within. Meeting the demands of the space within is a lot easier. You know when you have eaten, drunk, and slept enough. There are internal thresholds that tell you that you have reached your limit. There are no external thresholds. There is nothing built in that can curb human aggression; nothing to tell you that you are over the line.

Racially, you can never become too dominant. Absolute domination is what race demands. To meet the demand, you must fight for the dominant position. Only in the top position can you find peace in the forest of external life. No one can change this dynamic; race will not allow it.

Every human being seeks out an identity. The penchant for attachment compels us to do so. Identity brings order to our lives. To procure an identity, Americans enter the forest of external life. Here they purchase the dead trees of the race. These trees are very expensive. The asking price, which is non-negotiable, is body, mind, and spirit. After the purchase, the buyers realize that the tree does not belong to them; they belong to the tree—a tree that they can only use to decorate.

Even though a tree has been fashioned for you in your color and is awaiting your purchase, no one has to buy the dead trees of the race. No one has to reside in the forest of external life. My grandfather never did. Waights Tucker chose, instead, to pursue identity in the forest of internal life. Instead of attaching himself to the dead tree of the race, he attached herself to the family tree of life.

This was not something new. People lived for family long before America was founded. They were guided from within by custom and tradition handed down by their ancestors. These customs and traditions helped them develop qualities of faith, compassion, devotion, cleanliness, piety, dedication, integrity, honesty, austerity, humility, and love. Their struggle was not external; it was internal. Their perceptual reality, the place from whence they projected their identity, was found inside. They lived their lives facing inward. Family was the focal point. Living for the family is internal life. Living this life, the family maintains its internal connection.

This lifestyle is at odds with American culture. In this day and time giving oneself to family is primitive. Most Americans live for the race. The racial connection is valued more than the family connection. To be connected to the race, they live their lives facing outward.

Facing outward has its downside. It inhibits internal interaction. Facing outward, you cannot see what's going on internally. It's who you are internally that connects you to the family. To keep this connection active there must be internal interaction. This interaction does not take place instinctively; it requires conscious participation.

Prior civilizations were perpetuated by this principle. It was made operable by observing custom and tradition. The customs and traditions of the ancestors provided the blueprint for internal interaction. Following these ancient guidelines, the family could keep its internal connection active.

In America these customs and traditions have been abandoned. Having accepted race as its identity the family's internal connection has become inactive. The family has lost control of all of its faculties, the body, the mind, and the spirit. How the family interacts is determined by the race.

The space created by race only allows external interaction. It exists outside the family circle. In this space there is no internal interaction. Everyone is facing outward. From this position you can only pursue external life.

There are no family trees in the forest of external life. The only trees standing are the dead trees of the race. These trees are individual and produce nothing of substance. With no family tree to conjoin with, there is nothing to give life to the family within. In this environment there is only one family present, the family of the race.

The family of the race is the family of individuals. Everyone is identified externally. They live their lives outside the family circle. Their success is determined by how well they decorate their dead tree. The dead tree of the race is no substitute for the live tree of the family. No one has to settle for a dead tree. There is a live tree for everyone to claim. Every family has its tree. To find your family tree, you must face inward. Facing inward you can enter the forest of internal life.

The Forest of Internal Life

In this forest all of the trees have life; they produce seed, flowers, and fruit. The seed is the body, the flower is the mind, and the fruit is the spirit. Every family has a tree in the forest of internal life. To find your tree, the family must take up internal life. Internal life is the life you live for family. Living for the family, my grandfather found our family tree of life. In this place where the family tree resides, he formed a circle. Inside this circle is where he lived his life. Until now this place had not been identified. I call this place Humaria.

Humaria is not an external place. You will not find it on any map. Humaria is the place inside the family circle where the family tree resides.

My grandfather was known for tending trees. In his lifetime, he planted more than one thousand trees. He single-handedly transformed our family compound into a bountiful grove, replete with fruit bearing trees, exotic herbs, flowering bushes, and elegant shrubs. His creative genius was not only visible on the street that I grew up on; he left his mark all over Morganton, NC, a small rural town of eight thousand people. From the eastside to the westside, his mastery was on grand display. He enjoyed creating beautiful space and there was no space more beautiful than the space he created inside our family circle.

This space was special. It was special because he made it special. He frowned upon ugliness. He would not allow anything ugly inside the circle. In his mind, race was ugly. It was a divisive element that brought out the worst in people. To protect the family circle, he never allowed race inside. Sharing family for him was not sharing race. Our family was never identified as black. Black families had limitations. They had to go outside the family to find an identity.

My grandfather never looked outside the family for anything. He lived his life facing inward. His philosophy was: make the circle special and there will be no need for anyone to go outside. To make the circle special, he planted a garden and placed God in the center. He raised his family in the garden. There was no need to go outside to eat the forbidden fruit of the race. He knew that eating this forbidden fruit would turn the family outward.

When I was six years old, my grandfather told me a story about race that I never forgot. "We don't belong to a race," he said, "We belong to a family." All men are related; we all have a common father. The Indians have a great story that illustrates this.

The Family of Mankind

Once upon a time the Father of Mankind summoned his four sons, North, South, East, and West. He announced that it was time for them to go out to claim the directions. After embracing for the last time, the brothers were positioned back to back and sent off in the four directions. North had pale skin as he was formed from water; South had dark skin as he was formed from the earth; East had yellow skin as he was formed from gold; and West had red skin as he was formed from fire. The four sons departed never to see one another again.

In another place in the forest, the Earth Mother assembled her twelve daughters, January, February, March, April, May, June, July, August, September, October, November, and December, to announce that the time had come to populate the earth. Three daughters each were sent out in four directions. December, January, and February were sent North; March, April, and May were sent West; June, July, and August were sent South; and August, September, and October were sent East. After some time they met the four brothers who looked like them but were males. The four places they met became known as North, South, East, and West. Soon a family was produced, and from time to time they would talk around the fire about what life was like before they met. The men talked about their brothers and the women talked about their sisters. They were amazed to find so many similarities. After time, however, this knowledge of sisters and brothers was lost. When the descendants of the brothers and the sister reconnected they did not know that they were related. Now you know the secret and it's up to you to keep this knowledge alive.

A family facing outward loses contact with its core. It's from the core that the family derives its sustenance. To provide sustenance the core must have life. This life is personality. In my family, the personality was given life by my grandfather.

It was a reflection of his character, work ethic, integrity, decency, and humility, and it had no race. Although he has long passed away, that personality is still vibrant today. He infused it in all of his children. My mother came to embody its spirit. In her, this personality took on a whole new dimension. In my mother, the beauty that was my grandfather was made even sweeter. She gave the personality something that only a woman can give; she gave it a mother.

Our mother of Humaria carried on the custom that was started by her father. She kept race out of the family space. Facing inward she created space beyond race. In this space I found joy, peace, love, tenderness, warmth, protection, openness, charity, hope, understanding and forgiveness. In the circle she formed around the family tree, she also planted a garden. Unlike her father's garden where the family found succulent fruits and vegetables, in her garden the family found fragrant flowers. In this beautiful garden she welcomed all people. Anyone who chose to reside there could. No one was turned away because of race.

My mother knew no race. She lived her life inside the family circle. No matter where she was or what she was doing she never left Humaria. Although race was all around her it never drew her out. Her body, mind, and spirit were never lost to race. She never turned her back on the family tree of life.

In this tree she saw the mighty hands of God at work. From this tree, God gave the family seed, flowers, and fruit—the seed of the body, the flower of the mind, and the fruit of the spirit.

The family tree of life is God's creation, not man's. Unlike the manmade tree of the race, nothing external is required to sustain it. It derives its sustenance directly from God. Man has no control over what the family tree produces. The seed of the body, the flower of the mind, and the fruit of the spirit are crafted by God Himself.

Using these faculties, man is empowered to create space, internal and external. External space is the space created outside the family circle. This space is not operated for the benefit of the family; it's operated for the benefit of the race. Race controls external space. And nowhere is that control exercised more thoroughly than in America.

America is external space. To create this space Americans have been drawn out of the family circle by race. In America, the members of the family circle face

outward. Drawn out by race, the family has lost contact with its core. The space inside the family circle where the family tree resides is not being tended.

Every family has its Humaria, but not every family can claim it. What they claim instead is space outside of the circle where the trees of the race are found. To tend these trees the family must face outward. The body, mind, and spirit are used to cultivate space outside the family circle. This space is color coded black or white.

In this culture of racialism, living beyond race is a tremendous challenge but there are families who manage to do so. My family happens to be one of those. The life that we live is a tribute to my grandfather and mother. The space they created inside our family circle is so wonderful that no one has to go outside the family to pursue an identity. The space that we create is beyond race.

Action taken to create space beyond race is referred to here as Humarianism. Humarianism has two degrees of practice: the first and second degree. **The First Degree Practitioners** have allowed race to invade their family space. There was no one in the family strong enough to keep race out of the family circle. They identified with race, but in the presence of other races, they created space through acts of kindness that is beyond race. In this space there is opportunity for non-racial interaction. It rarely occurs because in most instances both parties cling to their racial identity during the exchange. Everything is done as a white person, black person, etcetera. Race is never left out of the equation. Compelled to protect their identity, they cannot take full advantage of the space that they create.

Not long ago I had an exchange with a **First Degree Practitioner.** Shortly after this exchange, I received the following email:

Dear Mr. Williams,

Some months ago I met you in the parking lot of St. Joseph's Hospital emergency room. I helped you change a woman's tire. You used a word which I found striking; if I remember, it was "Humarian," concerning my willingness as a white person to help a black person in need. I know I'm probably oversimplifying, but I found what you had to say to be quite moving and enlightening.

As we stand on the brink of having a black man in the white house being a conceivable reality (which would do the country as a whole a great deal of good), I think a lot about race relations. I feel I was raised to be tolerant and compassionate; my father participated in the Civil Rights Movement of the '60s, and was in Detroit during the '67 riots.

As I mentioned to you, I enjoy being a white person in Atlanta because black people are a majority, and I detect a sense of at-easeness with my fellow black Atlantans. This is in stark contrast with how I perceive blacks in my hometown in Michigan, where blacks are a minority (It's not Detroit, by the way). You made an interesting comment regarding transcending race, where blacks and whites could let go of their racial identity and simply exist together. I have thought a great deal about this concept, although I have not reached any conclusions.

I've also had some interesting additional input: I've made friends over the past few years with several Brazilians. It seems that Brazilians who are descendants of African slaves have a much different stature in Brazil than descendants of African slaves do in the U.S. There appears to be much more integration and harmony between ethnic groups in Brazil, although there are still class boundaries. In fact, my Brazilian friends are frequently puzzled as to why relationships between black and white in the U.S. have to be so complex and so confrontational. This gives me hope: if Brazil can have African slaves just as the U.S. did, and reach a point of acceptance that they have, then so can we. I hope. I remain truly grateful for our encounter (and also for the opportunity to help the woman who had a flat tire). I would really value a dialogue with you regarding race relations, and I think there's no better time for it. I crave perspective. Thanks for listening.

With respect and regards,

Ben Richards
Atlanta

There are millions of **First Degree Practitioners;** their votes elected President Obama. They show benevolence to members of other races, but in the presence of the race they identify with they seek racial privilege. As a consequence, the space that they create beyond race is only temporary.

To create permanent space the **First Degree Practitioner** must sever all racial ties. This is not possible for those who seek the benefits of racial privilege. For those in the dominant position, this is a major hurdle and there are no external rewards for doing it. In fact it may even lead to hardship. There is a price to pay for turning your back on the race. This is even true for those at the bottom, the people who use race as a shield rather than for domination.

No one can walk away from race, black or white, without suffering repercussions. Trying to withdraw, you quickly realize what an enormous stranglehold race has on the family. In some families, announcing that you have severed ties with God would be more acceptable than announcing that you have severed ties with the race. For the **First Degree Practitioner** who is willing to endure being ostracized, the rewards of the Second Degree of Humarianism await him.

To practice the Second Degree, the practitioner must expunge race from his psyche. Allowed to infiltrate the family circle, the family personality becomes race. Shedding this personality is no easy task; it requires an act of God. To help rid the family space of this personality, the Humarian Precept has been written.

The Humarian Precept

The Humarian Precept is a discipline that is designed to free the family from the bondage of race. The precept has as its core objective **the dismantling of racial identity.** The Humarian Precept is not a religion; it is a lifestyle that religions plagued by race can plug into. It creates space where the family can live beyond race.

By taking up this Humarian lifestyle, those who have allowed race to infiltrate their family space can be reconciled. From the Humarian perspective, giving oneself to race is a form of idolatry. God competes with the idol of the race for the hearts, minds, and souls of the family.

Families do things for the race that they never do for God. Race consciousness is more prevalent than God consciousness. Race has more influence on family than God. Out of ignorance, men approach God seeking blessings in the name of the race instead of the family.

God knows no race, but he does know family. Race has no relationship with God. God only claims the family of man. Race is man's invention. To give life to race, man defies God. He uses God to legitimize idol worship. Race takes the focus off God and places it on man. God is not race, and race is not God. Giving oneself to race is denying oneself to God. Tying God to race is blasphemy. Race is a captive state. Everyone ensnared is bound by the dictates of the race. God makes no dictates to the race; the behavior of the race is dictated by men, men who seek the power of racial domination. The pleasure they seek is not sought to please God, it is sought to please man. Seeking this pleasure, man has defied God. To atone for this offense, man must reconcile.

By God's grace, every family has a tree. From this tree the gifts of body, mind, and spirit are received. In this world there is nothing more precious than these "Three Gifts of God." Without them there would be no family experience.

God wants man to belong to a family but race will not allow it. Race is standing between God and man. Cloaked in the garb of the race, man approaches God as a white or black Christian, white or black Muslim, white or black Jew, and white or black Hindu, aspiring to be externally connected.

What you connect to God becomes an extension of God, according to the advocates of race. Pleasing the extension is no different than pleasing God. To please the extension, God bestows racial privilege. Those who believe this have been grossly misled. God does not bestow racial privilege. Racial privilege is not sought to please God, it is sought to please man. Why would God reward man's injustice to man?

The system of awarding racial privilege is man's creation, not God's. To be in a position to bestow racial privilege, you must also be in a position to deny it. It was for this purpose that the white race was formed. It was formed not only to extend privilege; it was formed to deny privilege. One cannot exist without the other. The people who formed the white race were inspired by greed, not by God. They gave their body, mind, and spirit to the race to turn a profit. This giving of oneself to the race slights God.

Everything given to the race belongs to the race even if it's given in God's name. You can dedicate yourself to the race in God's name and the race will accept you. Race has no shame. It pilfers God's glory. It tries to engage God in its preservation. Race will go to any length to promote itself. Considering this, why would God encourage a competitor?

Race competes with God for the hearts, minds, and souls of mankind. Among races, God's most fierce competitor is the white race. According to believers the preservation of whiteness is the highest calling, everyone should aspire to be white, even God. A God who is not white is unacceptable. Whiteness is the standard by which all things are to be judged. Under no circumstances should the preservation of whiteness be given up, not even for the sake of God.

Letting Go of Whiteness

God did not construct whiteness. Whiteness was sired in the minds of men. It was constructed to impose domination. The same minds that erected whiteness also erected blackness. One cannot exist without the other. They are both housed in the same structure. Whiteness occupies the top floor and blackness occupies the bottom.

To live in whiteness you must live above blackness. The people you live above must acknowledge that you are white. Having whiteness acknowledged is more about conceding space than it is about color. Nothing has done more to elicit recognition than placing things beyond the reach of blacks. The embrace of blackness is a response to being denied by whiteness. Being denied by whiteness imposes blackness. Whiteness created the space that blackness occupies and the people in the space can dismantle it. All they have to do to dismantle it is to let go of blackness. This will be no easy task. Those who live in whiteness will oppose it. With no one to claim the space at the bottom, the structure will eventually collapse. Blackness reinforces whiteness.

Blackness is not of African origin; it was constructed for African people by the architects of whiteness. Space was constructed for those pegged for domination. With no one to claim the space there would be no one to dominate. The domination that the white race enjoys is man's arrangement, not God's. God does not favor any race. Man, not God, created the racial divide.

What man does in whiteness or blackness is done for the glory of the race, not for the glory of God. And because man is the initiator, not God, it is the most difficult thing for man to give up. In this world nothing gives you greater access to power than whiteness. Having tapped into this power, why would you give it up? Is there something greater than whiteness? Yes, there is. But to realize this knowledge you must let go of whiteness. No man can do this on his own; only God can release man from the clutches of whiteness and blackness.

One way to petition God is to pray the **Prayer for Racial Extrication.** Living to preserve whiteness or blackness is not living for God. Living for God has nothing to do with race. This conclusion is the essence of the Humarian Precept. To adopt the precept those living in race consciousness should pray the **Prayer for Racial Extrication.**

The Prayer for Racial Extrication

Dear Lord, Most Merciful Father, I come to You this day with a humble heart, asking for Your forgiveness. I failed You, Lord, I did not receive the gifts of body, mind, and spirit, with an appreciative heart. Not only did I not receive these gifts in appreciation, I failed to thank You for them. I would like to thank You now.

Not receiving the gifts properly is not my only failing, Lord. My greatest failure has come from squandering them. Done unconsciously, I have given the gifts of body, mind, and spirit to the race. In doing so, I placed race above You. I have given more to the race than I have given to You. I allowed race to become Lord of my life.

All knowing and all loving God, please forgive my indiscretion. By Your mercy, I have come to see the error of my ways. It is to You, not the race, that I am indebted. With Your help I can turn myself around. Please help me Lord! Take back from the race the body, mind, and spirit that You have given me. I'm begging You, Lord, free me from the bondage of the race. Only You have the power to do so.

In the mood of love and appreciation, I have prepared my heart to receive the gifts. I understand their true purpose and I will accept them joyfully in celebration. With their possession, I will turn inward, away from the race. Facing inward I will create family space that has You in the center.

Bless me Lord so that I may bless my family. Please free me from the clutches of the race. In Your holy name I pray. Amen.

If God is so inclined, anyone who recites this simple prayer sincerely will be released from the clutches of the race. By God's grace the faculties of body, mind, and spirit will be returned to them. With the faculties fully recovered, one can create permanent space that is beyond race. The best place to create this space is inside the family circle. In this space one can practice the Second Degree of Humarianism.

To practice the second degree, the practitioner must live inside the family circle. To live inside the circle one must control the faculties of body, mind, and spirit. Having retained control, the faculties can be used to cultivate the garden.

The faculties of body, mind, and spirit were given by God through family, and should be given back to God through family. To give them back, the Second Degree Humarian takes care of the family garden.

10

Tending the Family Garden

To help the *Second Degree Humarian* stay internally connected, three tools have been crafted. These tools keep the focus of identity fixed on who you are internally and act as portals that allow access to family space. Family space is internal. To be active in this space you must be internally connected. The family has three lineal connections, through body, mind, and spirit.

Body   **Mind**   **Spirit**

Using these tools the **Second Degree Humarian** can cultivate the space inside the family circle. The space inside the circle is a garden. In this garden there is a tree that produces the family jewels: the seeds of the body, the flowers of the mind, and the fruits of the spirit. To take up the process of cultivation, the Second Degree Humarian should begin with the fruit.

The Fruit of the Spirit

The family has three lineal connections: the seed connects the bodies, the flower connects the minds, and the fruit connects the spirit. Of the three connections, the spiritual connection is the most essential. It is through cultivating the fruit of the spirit that the family comes to love God. It was for this purpose that the family was created. With no love of God there is no family. God will not allow it. Why should He? Why would God sanction something that is structured to defy Him? Family that is not about God is not family. The family of the race is not family. Race cannot offer family. Only God offers family. The only thing that race offers that God does not is racial domination. To acquire this power, man puts race before God and family.

Man loves the race above all things and filters everything through the race, including God.

However, there is only one God and that God is not the race. God competes with race for the soul of the family and there are millions of families who have lost their souls to the race.

It was in this area that my grandfather and mother made their greatest contribution. Race never got a foothold in the family because they instilled in their children the love of God. Nothing gives more life to the family circle. To qualify to parent you must instill love of God. You instill love of God when you cultivate the fruit of the spirit. The cultivation produces its greatest yield when it takes place inside the family circle.

Cultivation is not limited to any one process. Love of God is available through numerous faith perspectives. No one religion has a lock on love of God.

Spirit

At different times and in different places, personalities have appeared who claimed to be God or God's representative. Yahweh, Krishna, Moses, Christ, Mohammed, Bahá'u'lláh, and Buddha are among them. If it were announced today that these personalities were going to reappear simultaneously in Atlanta, what percentage of the world's population would flock there to greet them? I imagine that it would be the largest gathering of lovers of God in the history of mankind.

If during the gathering, an appeal was made for all lovers of God to come forward and choose one personality, which personality would everyone choose? Considering that humanity is not monolithic, is there any personality that can attract the whole of mankind? As of today, that personality has not yet appeared. No personality appearing as God or God's messenger has attracted everyone. If these personalities appeared in a public forum, could any one of them claim that He alone attracted all of the spectators? It's highly unlikely such a claim would be made. The reason being that attraction is not something that anyone controls, not even God. If attraction were controlled, love would not exist. To love, you must have the power of rejection. We reject things that hold no attraction. If someone controlled attraction, rejection would not be possible.

The first principle of love is attraction. To love, there must be some attraction. To become the object of attraction, God reveals Himself to man; man cannot approach God. If it were God's desire to not be known, no man would know Him. To be known, God approaches man in two ways: He comes Himself or He sends His messenger. In doing so He runs the risk of being rejected. It's by God's wishes that all men have the power to reject Him. History shows that every personality that has appeared on earth as God or God's messenger has faced rejection. The degree of rejection varies, but it would be measurable in a forum where each personality made an individual appeal for followers.

To date, no single personality, no single act, no single offering, and no single religion has attracted the whole of mankind. In every attempt made to establish religion, the rejection was greater than the acceptance. When mortals are rejected they feel pain. With this in mind just try to imagine what God feels. Does God have feelings? Some say no. They believe man has something that God does not have. How can you love and not have feelings? God loves us so much that He exposes Himself to rejection. Knowing this, it's only logical to assume that the sin of rejection is perhaps the source of God's greatest pain.

To show His love, Yahweh bestowed upon Adam and Eve His likeness, freedom from all pain and suffering, dominion over all the earth, free association, and immortality. His mission was to establish heaven on earth. Had Adam and Eve not eaten the forbidden fruit, they could have lived on earth forever. Every child they conceived in the Garden would have been born immortal. The Earth planet that Yahweh created was a planet of life; it was not created to be a planet of death. Rejection in the form of disobedience triggered the response that transformed the planet of life into the planet of death. In the process, Adam and Eve suffered the greatest loss in human history. They lost their immortality. Could it be that they had to suffer loss before they could love?

Krishna was also rejected. From the moment He appeared there were those who sought his annihilation.

The purpose of His appearance was to protect His devotees. Krishna spoke the following words, "There is no truth superior to Me. Everything rests upon me as pearls are strung on a thread. I am the taste of water, the light of the sun and the moon. I am the sound in ether, the ability in man, the original fragrance of the earth, and the heat in fire. I am the life of all that lives." After declaring these things boldly on the battlefield, Krishna gave the enemies of His devotees an opportunity to surrender. They refused to surrender and a great war ensued that led to their annihilation.

Perhaps Christ suffered the most brutal form of rejection. His mission was to bring salvation, the gift of eternal life, to the Jewish people. To attract them He performed miracles. He walked on water, turned water into wine, made a blind man see, and brought a dead man back to life. His miracles attracted multitudes but failed to earn Him what He desired most: the overwhelming love and devotion of all His people. After all else failed, He made the ultimate sacrifice; He gave up His life. This, too, proved insufficient. Giving up His life did not earn Him acceptance as the Jewish Messiah. In the end, He was rejected by people He came to save.

Mohammed, too, had to face rejection. His mission was one of peace but His efforts to promote peace were met with open hostility. The ramifications from His rejection still linger today; they have not been reconciled. Rejection made eternal enemies out of those He termed the infidels. The infidels rejected His teachings, threatened His life, and would not allow Him to preach openly. It was in response to them that He picked up the sword. None of this would have been necessary if attraction were controlled. Because it is not controlled, the personalities who have represented themselves as God and His messenger have all suffered rejection. No one wants rejection, but rejection is something that all religions have had to contend with.

Man has free will, which allows him to pick and choose. Not all men have the same taste. When approaching them, God and His Messenger must contend with different preferences. There are men who will only accept a Black God and men who will only accept a white God. There are also those who will only accept an angry God, and those who only accept a God of peace. For others, God must be formless, and still others who prefer a God with form. Our acceptance of God is conditional. As such, no one personality has been able to satisfy all men. To do so would be a contradiction; one personality would have to be black and white, angry and peaceful, have form and be formless. To avoid the pretext for such contradictions, different personalities of Godhead have appeared.

All men are not on the same level and you find them in all religions. There are those who ask nothing of God but to serve Him. They are willing to go anywhere and accept any condition just for the opportunity to serve. Just hearing the glories of God in the company of likeminded souls gives them complete satisfaction. Their prayer is simple: "My dear Lord, do with me as You please. I am a soul surrendered unto You. Use me as your doormat if You please; my love for You is unconditional. Serving You is my only ambition." For such souls the attraction is the personality of God, not what He has to offer. Service opportunities are all they require. Others, however, only respond to gifts. To get their attention, some benediction such as prosperity has to be bestowed. Others have no interest in gifts or service; the only thing they respond to is fear. To get their attention, fear has to be provoked. One way to provoke fear is to issue a threat, such as, "If you don't accept Me as your Lord and Savior, I will condemn you to hell eternally." Threats like this provoke fear, but fear has no quality of attraction. You cannot love someone or something that you fear may destroy you. If God held a gun to your head and demanded love, that love would not be real. No one can be forced to love. Acting to avoid hell is no different than acting to avoid a bullet. The action is motivated by fear. To love God, it must be voluntary and without any fear of reprisal. Fearing God is not the same as loving God; it's not something you choose to do. Fear, although a great motivator is no substitute for love. God wants our love. He wants us to love Him more than He wants us to fear Him. But there are those who can only be reached by fear; they accept God to avoid suffering.

The last group, those on the lowest level, cannot be reached at all. No service, gifts, or threats are able to move the 150 million-plus atheist in the world today. Using the free will that God has given them, they reject Him. That rejection is the price God pays for love. To purchase our love, He opens Himself up to rejection, which further proves that no one controls attraction.

God does not control attraction but He is the most attractive. He alone possesses all of the qualities of attraction. He is the most beautiful, the most intelligent, the wealthiest, the strongest, and the most benevolent. God is the origin of everything and no one is more worthy of love. What we find attractive in others is but a spark of His splendor. God is unlimited and as such His unlimited nature cannot fully manifest in this limited material world. Even if it did, our limited perception would not allow us to view it.

Unlike God, we are not omnipresent, our eyes and ears are not everywhere. Even if they were, we would not be able to process all the information they gathered. Our perception is limited; we can only view God through one stationary lens. Because our perception is limited we are unable to perceive God in His totality. As a result, different personalities of Godhead are being pitted against one another. God is doing battle with God within the body of man. We resolve the conflict when we realize that the one God has innumerable forms and personalities. The conflict arises when we try to place limitations on God. Different religions represent different aspects of the one God. No one religion represents God in His entirety; they are but pieces of the same pie.

God's forms, personalities, and benedictions are three factors that influence our faith. There is, however, a fourth factor that is even more significant, and that is our birth. Our birth plays the greatest role in determining our faith. Most of us did not choose our faith; the family imposed it upon us. Few people take the opportunity to study different religions and then choose one based on their findings. If you were born in a Christian family, more than likely you will become a Christian. The same is true for other religions. With that said, it's important to recognize the role that the family plays.

Religion took birth in the family. The family is the oldest institution and the first to receive knowledge of God. No institution does more to preserve religion. God does not choose the members of the church, mosque, temple, or synagogue, but He does choose the members of the family.

The fruit of the spirit was not given to any one religion it was given to the family to develop. In choosing a family, God knows what religion is being practiced. The family religion is the religion that most people adopt. Nothing has a greater spiritual influence than the family. Being placed by God in the family of Christians, Muslims, Hindus, Jews, Buddhist, etcetera, is a Divine arrangement that seems to suggest that all religions have a Divine purpose. Within all of them we find lovers of God.

Humarianism is not an advocate of any one religion. Any religion that has race issues can plug in. Humarianism does not contradict any religious teachings; it does, however, recommend that couples share the same faith perspective. The mixing of faiths complicates bonding. The goal is to become one being in spirit. Divisions of faith are difficult to reconcile because there is no room for compromise. Christians should marry Christians, Muslims should marry Muslims, Jews should marry Jews, and Hindus should marry Hindus. Sharing the same faith perspective is critical when creating the spiritual bond.

Before bonding physically and mentally, couples should bond spiritually. To bond, they must give up their independence and share the same spiritual identity. To share identity, they must do things together to please God. A regiment of praise and worship, working as volunteers to help the elderly, homeless, and handicapped, and the study of scripture, is a good way to initiate a relationship.

Doing things together to please God they get a sense of who they are in the spirit. With this knowledge they can determine their spiritual compatibility. Having determined compatibility they can petition God to create a spiritual bond between them. This bonding constitutes the first marriage, the marriage of the spirit. To honor this union, a private ceremony should be performed in which prayers are offered by both parties asking God to create the bond. Vows should also be exchanged, promising never to break them. With the spiritual bond established, the marriage of the bodies and the minds should follow.

The Seed of the Body

There are two ways to view the seed—external and internal. Viewed externally, the seed is not viable until after conception. Prior to conception there is no recognition of life. Viewed externally, there are only four phases of the human evolutionary growth process: gestation, childhood, adolescence, and adulthood. The first phase of the process, pre-conception is ignored. The production of seed is not viewed as a major reproductive function. This however is not the case when the seed is viewed from the internal perspective.

When viewed internally, the body first appears as a seed. The initial generation of human life, nascence, occurs when the molecules that compose the seed are activated by consciousness. The combination of consciousness and inert matter engenders the seeds of life. These seeds are the first conscious elements of human existence to manifest.

Inert molecules have no quality or sense of existence and thus have no ability to expand consciousness. This suggests that consciousness exists before the molecules are assembled into seed form. This expansion of consciousness is the defining principle of human reproduction and is a phenomenon that occurs within the body of man. The first symptoms of human life are exhibited by seeds, which display the first awareness of existence and true sense of purpose.

This exhibition of purpose is the first demonstration of human intelligence. Upon discharge, the seed seeks out the egg for fertilization, which illustrates an awareness of existence and purpose. The seed not only has awareness, it also has form—a head and a tail that provides mobility. The egg, unlike the seed, is unconsciousness and does not display any symptoms of life. There is no awareness of existence or purpose, and no mobility. The egg cannot seek out the seed; the seed must seek out the egg to bring it to life and be activated with consciousness. For that reason, the seed has been chosen to represent the body.

The seed appears in the body of man, which indicates that the paternal relationship is the first to manifest. Your father had the first opportunity to claim you as kin because you first appeared as a male or female seed in his body. Because it was your father that produced the seed your relationship with him preceded your relationship with your mother. Any woman could have received the seed, but only one man could produce it—your father. His identity as your father was fixed when he produced the seed. He produced the seed before you had a mother.

We evolve our male and female identity from the seed produced by our father. Our father's identity also evolves from the seed that he produces. A man can cultivate a relationship with his seed before he has contact with a woman if he chooses. This by no means minimizes the role that women play. The seed can only realize its true purpose by fertilizing an egg that is produced by the female. No attempt is made here to diminish the contribution that

Body

women make. Our goal is to establish the order in which human relationships evolve.

The First Mother

The first parental relationship established is paternal in nature and is referred to here as the lineage of the body. The lineage of the body is the family's kinship connection with its seed. The kinship community is expanded each time a seed is produced. It is the duty of every male who reaches puberty to keep the seed inside the family circle. This is done by identifying the seed as family. ***The seed belongs to the family.*** God did not give that seed to an individual; he gave it to the family. Every family member is connected to it. The men who understand this and cultivate a relationship with the seed as family property are patriarchs.

In families who allow the seed to be disconnected, there are no patriarchs prior to conception. The seed is not accorded kinship until a pregnancy occurs. Before pregnancy occurs, these men allow the seed to be driven outside the family circle. Possession is not maintained on behalf of the family. The lineal relationship that is established by its production is considered null and void. The internal connection between the family and the seed is mentally disconnected. Prior to and after conception the seed assumes the status of excrement.

Waste material cannot be tied to a lineal tradition. It cannot be used to consciously perpetuate human life. Its perception as excrement will not allow it to assume that role. The only role that it can credibly play is that of a spoiler, a non-entity that causes an unintended pregnancy. Nowhere has this perception had a more devastating impact on the lineage of a population than on those who live for the black race in America.

The lineal connection with the seed has three states: active, inactive, and dichotomized. The process used to perpetuate life determines the state that the lineage assumes. There are two ways to perpetuate human life, consciously and unconsciously. Those who live for the race procreate unconsciously. Their sexual unions have no lineal intent because kinship with the seed is not recognized until pregnancy occurs. The seed is regarded as excrement. There is no expectation during union other than an organism.

Because orgasm is the only expectation, it is not at all uncommon to find women who live for the race having intercourse with numerous men. To please these women, a man must spill his seed. When a pregnancy occurs in this environment and the father cannot be identified because there are numerous men, the lineage becomes dichotomized. The lineage is cut off because the child cannot be connected to the father that produced the seed.

When the father's identity is known but his conceptions are unintended, the lineage assumes an inactive state. Knowing the father's identity keeps the lineage intact, but that alone cannot keep the lineage active. To activate the lineage, the men in the family must claim the seed for the family and regulate its proliferation. The men who take up this practice live the life of a *Nu-Patriarch.*

The life of the *Nu-Patriarch* is internal. These men draw their identity from the line, not the race. They carry the seed with great awe and reverence. They take serious the responsibility of keeping the lineage active. To do so, they plan all their conceptions. When they plant the seed, they do so with conscious intent for the expressed purpose of expanding the line.

Among those who represent the black race in America, recent findings show that less than ten percent of the men plan conceptions. Because the seed is kept outside the family circle more than ninety percent of the pregnancies that they induce are unintended. Thirty-six percent of these unintended pregnancies end in abortion, and of the sixty-four percent that survive the womb, seventy percent are born out of wedlock.

What these findings tell us is that the perpetuation of human life by men who represent the black race is not driven by the desire for family. There are very few *Nu-Patriarchs.* The appearance of family for the most part is in the form of an imposition. Impositions are sometimes viewed as intrusions and require making adjustments. Having not made these adjustments some five million people living for the black race do not know the identity of their biological father.

If paternal intent were required for procreation, the same people might be on the verge of extinction. This calamitous situation is not something new; it has existed since the time of slavery. During slavery, the family's connection with its seed was severed. The slave owner took possession of the seed and controlled its proliferation. The breeding of slaves destroyed the institution of fatherhood. The position of the patriarch, so prevalent in African society, was abandoned. The connection to the ancestral root was cut off and new lines were never re-established.

In families that were formed during slavery there was no life in the family circle. Since that time, population growth has been fueled by the erotic exploits of boys in manly dress, boys who view the seed as excrement. Because they allow the seed to be debased, the paternal environment they create is totally dysfunctional.

Human life enjoys the highest value when it is conceived with conscious intent. Because there is no life inside the family circle those who represent the black race have no tradition of planning conceptions. The family as an institution does not take an active role in its formation. There is no custom observed that connects the family to its seed. Without such a custom, family lineage cannot be re-activated.

To adopt a lineal tradition, the family has to be structured and operated as an institution. These institutions are not being formed because family sovereignty has been relinquished to the race. Bereft of its sovereignty, the family has become a stooge for racial exploitation. Racial posturing has caused the lineal infrastructure to collapse. The internal damage is enormous but no one sees it; the family is facing outward.

When you are living outside the family circle everything you do is external, including your sex life. Sexuality viewed externally is a form of relief. This relief takes place outside the realm of family. Although hyped and glamorized as lovemaking, the base consciousness that induces external sex life is getting relief. For a man getting relief is about eliminating seminal waste.

Defecation for Procreation

When you rely on defecation for procreation, the process of creating human life is no different than urinating or having a bowel movement. If the object is to defecate, what difference does it make if it's urine, feces, or semen? The only difference is that latter is more stimulating than the others.

When the pressure builds, men who live for the race seek relief in the form of an orgasm. To accommodate these men, women who live for the race allow their bodies to be used as waste disposals. They render this service in hopes that they may also get relief in the process. All of this takes place outside the realm of family.

Viewed externally, what a man and woman do sexually is done for the individual, not for the family. Sexual unions by those who live for the race are not considered family functions. They take place beyond the sphere of family influence. As long as sexuality is kept outside the realm of family, the family cannot take any active role in its formation. With no procreative input, the family cannot be structured to function as a lineal institution.

To realize its full potential as the most powerful institution on earth the family must control its expansion. This can only be done internally. To take up this endeavor the family must give up its predilection towards race. It is from the seed, not the race, that the family draws its identity. The seed is the true origin of identity. The energy that produces the seed is internal and the identity manifested by the seed is kinship, not race.

Forming the Race

Man is related to every seed that he produces. Tying race to the seed is a diabolical scheme that was designed to undermine the institution of family. According to the scheme a white male produces white seed. If that seed is planted in a white female the seed remains white, but if it's planted in a black female the seed becomes black. Because the white seed has become black, the white family has no obligation to claim kinship.

Maintaining the integrity of the race is more important than maintaining the integrity of the family. This is a vivid example of how the family seed has been lost to the race. Who does the seed belong to? The family or the race? If you answer race, you see firsthand how the institution of family has been undermined.

The formation of the race takes place outside the family. The family has no control over who belongs to the race. It connects the family to people whose behavior cannot be regulated. Just because someone looks like you, does not make him or her fit for association. There is a price you pay to represent the race. You become a part of something that cannot be controlled.

The energy that creates race is external and is beyond the control of the family. No matter what you do, whether you rape your mother or kill your father, no one can kick you out of the race. Why would the family want to be identified with something that cannot be regulated?

Because the energy that creates race flows from the outside in, families that have no internal perspective cannot oppose it. The form that race takes is beyond the family's ability to mold. Identified racially, the family is forced to defend things that it has no control over.

The family can, however, control what it produces internally. The energy that produces the seed flows from the inside out and does not rely on external stimuli. Using custom and tradition, the family can control the proliferation of its seed. But held captive by what the external energy has produced in the form of race, the family cannot exercise any internal control.

The race dictates how the family handles its seed. The race tells the families who live for the white race that your seed is white. *If that seed is planted in a black woman, it becomes black and the white race will not accept it.* To live for the white race, the white family must accept this dictate. Who decided that the sovereignty of the white race should reign above the sovereignty of the family? Was it God? It certainly was not the family. Following the behavior dictated by the race, the family has been undermined.

That which controls behavior, controls expansion. The premise that the seed is a form of excrement has also been dictated by the race. To expand the race, sex outside of marriage is encouraged. Children born out of wedlock may have issues of identity within the family but there are no issues of identity with the race unless the parents are interracial. The white race only accepts children that are born of two white parents. This, however, is not an issue with the black race.

Children fathered by a white father and black mother are accepted by the black race. Children fathered by a black father and white mother are also accepted. Who decided that these children would be accepted? Who decided that the race would accept pre-marital sex, child molestation, and abortion? Having submitted to the dictates of the race, the family is forced to defend behavior that is an abomination before God. Although implicated by the behavior, the family has no say in what the race dictates.

Nothing has a greater impact on how the family is formed than how it views its seed. The race views the seed as waste material, and since race was introduced the seed has been under siege. The energy that produced race is at odds with the energy that produces the seed. There is a fierce struggle between the external and internal energy. So that race might reign supreme, the seed has been reduced in status to excrement. Waste material has no sovereignty. It cannot be used to free the family from racial bondage.

Lineal Injunction

To realize the intrinsic value of the seed, the family must keep its lineal connection with the body active.

This requires a lineal injunction. A lineal injunction is a regulatory principle that controls the proliferation of the seed. Different injunctions have been employed based on the desired objective. To preserve racial purity, an injunction was employed to **prohibit sex with members of another race.** To restore the integrity of the seed, one might employ an injunction that **reserves the first sexual encounter for procreation.** The goal here is to enhance the value of the seed by ensuring that the expansion of the family takes place intentionally.

Family expansion controlled by the flow of external energy, such as race, at best is incidental. Accidents cannot maintain the integrity of the seed. When the seed is viewed as excrement there is no impetus to regulate its proliferation. As a consequence, the family's internal connection becomes dichotomized or inactive. The internal energy that sustains the family within cannot flow freely. To regulate the flow, sexuality must be brought back into the realm of family. It must be conducted in a way that activates the lines. To activate the lines conceptions must be planned.

To determine how many lines are active, a **Family Diagnostic Evaluation** has to be performed. The **Family Diagnostic Evaluation** tells you how much life there is in the family circle. If none of the conceptions in your family were planned, there are no active lines. What this means is that there is no life in the family circle. Everyone is facing outward. Family life, which includes sexuality, is being performed outside the family circle. To bring life back into the circle, the seed must be connected to the family. To connect the seed, all conceptions must be planned.

Families that have no planned conceptions have no life in the family circle. The lineal connection to the seed is inactive. To give new life to the circle, a lineal injunction must be issued. To put the injunction into action it will require the efforts of a *Nu-Patriarch.*

A *Nu-Patriarch* is a man who brings new life to the family circle. To accomplish this mission, he acknowledges that he carries life in the form of a seed and plants that seed with love and conviction to revive the family lineage. The *Nu-Patriarch* lives for the line. Living for the line is not living for the race. Living for the line is living for the family. To live for the family, you must be facing inward. Facing inward you are always conscious of the lines.

Families that have no active lines are internally dead. To resuscitate a line, a relationship must be cultivated with the seed. The men who are in the best position to cultivate this relationship are those who have not become sexually active. This relationship cannot be established if the seed has been relegated to the status of waste material.

The spilling of the seed for recreation conditions the mind to view it as bodily waste. Once a man becomes comfortable spilling the seed, it is almost impossible to restore its integrity. For this reason, the *Nu-Patriarch* has to come from the ranks of men who have not become sexually active. The focus has to be fixed on the first sexual encounter. This event must be reserved to re-activate the family lineage. Without cultivating a relationship with the seed prior to the first sexual encounter, this is highly unlikely to occur.

The production of seed is the morphological function that perpetuates family lineage. Its production requires no conscious mental or physical endeavor on the part of the producer. The lineal function that produces the male and female seed is not external and as such is beyond man's control. This activity is controlled internally by nature.

No man has an awareness of how many male or female seeds he produces, so their appearance goes unheralded. To become notable, their appearance has to be tied to something tangible. Identifying the seed as male and female does not go far enough. Proper recognition is given when the seeds are identified as family.

The foundation on which human identity is built is kinship. Kinship is not a by-product of gender. Kinship and gender are manifested simultaneously. If kinship is not recognized, the gender of the seed cannot connect it to the family. Everyone who shares the same gender is not related. Kinship crosses gender lines. Lineage establishes kinship not gender.

Lineage produces the male and female seed, but interaction with the seed as family is not possible until the seed is identified as a potential son or daughter. The lineal connection becomes active when kinship with the seed is recognized. Until kinship is acknowledged, no lineal interaction can take place. Only after kinship with the seed is established can one live for the line.

To become a *Nu-Patriarch,* a man must identify every seed he produces as a potential son or daughter and plan all of his conceptions. A planned conception is a sexual union agreed to by married partners to expand the line. The motivation for taken up this endeavor is to bring life to the family circle.

Resurrecting the Line

To enjoy the greatest success, this mission has to be taken up before the first sexual encounter. There is no greater service a man can perform for his family than that of resurrecting the line. In order to perform this noble act a man requires a *Nu-Matriarch.*

The role of the *Nu-Patriarch* in this regard is of paramount importance, but even more important is the role of the *Nu-Matriarch.* The lineage has to flow through a woman. The woman who receives the seed that activates the lineage is the *Nu-Matriarch,* the new mother of the line.

There are three functions at work in the universe: creation, maintenance, and destruction. It takes more energy to maintain the universe than it does to create or destroy it. The patriarch creates the seed and transfers it. The matriarch receives the seed and maintains it. By allowing it to flow through her she preserves the lineage.

Not all women are qualified to preserve the lineage. Like the *Nu-Patriarch,* the *Nu-Matriarch* should be a virgin and have a clear understanding of how her female identity evolved. Male and female identity evolves from the seed that is produced by man. The human evolutionary process is initiated by the production of seed. This morphological function takes place inside the body of a man and it produces the X and Y chromosomes. Female identity evolves from the Y chromosome.

Any woman who accepts the fact that her female identity evolved from seed produced by her father has the aptitude required to become a *Nu-Matriarch.* Because she can see the *Nu-Patriarch* internally, she can claim the space inside the family circle. Claiming the space, she can have a relationship with his seed.

Women who view the seed as excrement are not qualified. They cannot see the *Nu-Patriarch* as a paternal being. They cannot bring life to the family circle. Their interest in sexuality for the most part is recreational. For this reason they allow men to use their bodies as waste disposals. Sober women who have been trained to respect the seed find such behavior appalling. Only among them is there hope of finding a *Nu-Matriarch.*

Any man who seriously pursues a spouse to restore the family lineage will see all women as maternal beings. His mission as a *Nu-Patriarch* will not allow him to see women otherwise. Because he sees a maternal being, he can share intimacy with her inside the family circle as the potential mother of his child.

Women who live outside the family circle and have come to view the seed as excrement cannot respond properly to this intimacy. Because they have only known sex outside the family circle, they cannot see that the *Nu-Patriarch's* intentions are different from other men.

The best candidates for *Nu-Matriarch* are women who are chaste. Chastity is the symbol of feminine virtue. Only chaste women should be allowed inside the family circle. They are uniquely qualified to receive intimacy as maternal beings. Because they have had no sexual involvement they have no difficulty responding to a man who assumes the role of *Nu-Patriarch.* In these men they have access to opportunities that other men cannot offer them—the opportunity to become a *Nu-Matriarch,* the mother of the line.

Only a **Nu-Patriarch** can award the position of **Nu-Matriarch** to his spouse. The highest honor one can attain in family life is that of **Nu-Patriarch** and **Nu-Matriarch;** these positions can only be held by those who live inside the family circle.

In families that live for the race, there is no **Nu-Patriarch** or **Nu-Matriarch.** No one aspires for these positions because the seed is kept outside the family circle. If someone assumed the role of **Nu-Patriarch** and **Nu-Matriarch,** in such families they would go unrecognized.

Action taken to restore the lineage in families that live for the race might be contested. Family members who have always lived facing outward may oppose giving life to the family circle. Those addicted to sex life outside the circle may find sex life inside the circle too restrictive. The mere suggestion of such a thing may be viewed as a condemnation of their lifestyle.

Making one's intensions known to those who live for the race can pose a risk. If opposition arises, the **Nu-Patriarch** and **Nu-Matriarch** should not yield to intimidation. Any objection based on ignorance should be totally dismissed and not allowed to become a distraction. Activating the new line has to be the top priority. All it takes is two people to give life to the family circle.

The first duty of the **Nu-Matriarch** is to cultivate a relationship with the seed of her spouse. It is from her relationship with his seed that she draws her identity. The **Nu-Matriarch** is more than a spouse; she is the mother of the line. The lineage flows through her. To establish this relationship the seed must come into her possession. There are two ways to transfer the seed— mentally and physically. The mental process is referred to here as *mental copulation.* The process does not require physical contact. The procedure is purely psychological; interaction only takes place in the mind. The projection device used for the transfer is the tool that represents the seed.

The tool has to be configured before it can be used. The first step in the procedure is to attach the family name. The name connects the family to its seed. The tool used in this procedure represents the lineage. The lineage cannot be identified without a name. By attaching a name to the tool it becomes a Johnson, Williams, Smith, etcetera. With the family name attached, the lineal relationship can be affirmed.

Every seed a man produces is either male or female. The relationship with the seed is affirmed when it is identified as a son or daughter.

The tool is configured when the family name is attached and its gender is assigned. Meditating on the tool after it has been configured triggers an image of the child in the mind of the *Nu-Patriarch* and *Nu-Matriarch.* Attachment to this image unleashes emotions that create the parental bond that activates the lineage. No greater exchange of intimacy can occur between a man and woman than that which takes place when they commit to living for the line. When they fully understand the magnitude of what they are doing, they are overcome with the anxiety of anticipation. This anxiety will increase each day until it's time to physically conceive.

There are two phases of what is referred to here as the Lineal Procreation Procedure (L.P.P.): pre-conception and gestation. Pre-conception is the phase just prior to conjugation. Those who keep the seed outside the family

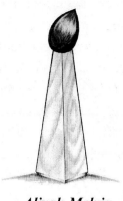

Aliyah Melvin

circle are unable to observe this because they view the seed as waste material. To participate in the first phase of the L.P.P., the seed must be kept inside the family circle. During this phase, the *Nu-Matriarch* has an opportunity to prepare herself physically and psychologically to receive the seed.

The *Nu-Matriarch* is best described as the preserver of the line, and to begin preservation she must take control of her space inside the family circle. A mother is someone who prepares and controls space. The first space a woman in the role of the *Nu-Matriarch* must take control of is the space inside her body. Nature has designed that space for the specific purpose of reproduction, and it is her duty as the *Nu-Matriarch* to maintain its viability. How she maintains her inner space reflects her understanding of maternity. To control this space requires a plan, but no plan will be effective if her sexual objectives are skewed.

Feminine space is most productive when it's used to preserve the line. Before it's used, however, it should be prepared for habitation. Becoming a **Nu-Matriarch** is a serious proposition, and it's essential that women prepare physically and psychologically to conceive. This may require the assistance of a physician. Tests are highly recommended to establish fertility prospects. Women who are unaware that they are infertile but engage in the process of reproduction run the risk of becoming depressed. It is best for them to know what their prospects of fertility are.

Preparing physically also involves proper diet, exercise, and the elimination of toxins from the body. A program for colon detoxification and blood purification should be undertaken one month before conception. Cigarettes, alcohol, and other drugs should be eliminated to help the body absorb essential nutrients. Eliminating toxins helps to transform the female body into a stockpile of nutrients for the child. Fasting is one of the most effective means of eliminating toxins. Fasting cleanses the body and enables a woman to take control of her inner space. Psychological preparation involves developing the proper mindset to receive the seed.

The best time for a woman to receive the seed is during the most fertile time of the month. This should be determined before a date is chosen for procreation. The best time to conjugate is between the twelfth and sixteenth day following the first day of the menstrual cycle.

Setting the date for conjugation is the most critical step in the pre-conception process. This action prepares the heart for procreation. The announcement acts as seed planted in the heart of the male and female that confirms their commitment to the preservation of the line. Immediately upon setting the date for conjugation, the waves of procreative emotions begin to flow. These emotions inspire deep introspection, which help prepare the mind for conjugation.

Of the three—heart, mind, and body—the mind is the most difficult to prepare. The mind is always subject to change and may question the decision to procreate. One way to keep it focused is through meditation. The *Nu-Patriarch* and *Nu-Matriarch* should meditate together on the symbolic seed. This meditation should begin the day the conjugation date is chosen.

This meditation is mental copulation, as it enables the seed to be planted in the mind of the potential mother before it is planted in her body. Carrying the seed in her mind arouses maternal affection, which indicates that she is ready to receive the seed in its physical form.

The *Nu-Patriarch* must also prepare to plant the seed. The rudiments of fatherhood do not develop through spontaneous revelation. There must be a period of preparation; choosing a time to conceive gives the prospective father an opportunity to make the necessary psychological adjustments.

The desire to procreate manifests itself only in the mind of a man who is driven by a purpose. This purpose is garnered from the process of self-evaluation. Through this process a man can determine what qualities and resources he possesses that are worthy of being passed on to future generations. The temper of his purpose is illustrated by the willingness to allocate space in his life for a child. This allocation of space refers to time, and the paternal clock starts ticking when the seed is released. At least fifteen days of preparation are required before a man should release his seed.

During this fifteen-day period of preconception, daily meditation should be conducted to affirm the purpose and potential of the seed. The meditation should be conducted twice daily, morning and evening, and it should consist of silence and a recitation that acknowledges the potential and purpose of the seed and the egg. A sample recitation for the male is as follows: "The seed in my body is the origin of life; through it I expand the lineage." A sample recitation for the female is: "The egg in my body is the preserver of life; through it I expand the lineage." This recitation should be repeated fifteen times during each session and should be preceded by two minutes of silent meditation.

The effects of the meditation will be felt immediately. Parental anxiety in the form of anticipation will start to build and it will intensify until conjugation. This anxiety creates a parental bond between the potential father and mother and it intensifies until the preconception period is complete.

The next phase of the growth process is gestation. The gestation period begins when the seed is planted. For those who have no parental aspirations, the beginning of the gestation period cannot be noted. The planting of the seed is done for the purpose of recreation and there is no transition from preconception to gestation.

When the purpose of the union is recreation, no parental bonding takes place until conception is confirmed. Bonding cannot take place because the anticipated outcome of the act is not conception. The physical bonding that occurs, although extremely exhilarating, has a very short lifespan even if it lasts all night. The most enduring bond is psychological. When the psychological attributes of sex life are compared to the physical, the two cannot be equated.

When the purpose of the first sexual encounter is procreation, the impression that is left in the mind can last a lifetime. One of the strongest bonds that can exist between a man and woman is created when they share sexual intimacy during the first sexual encounter to conceive a child. A couple is given only one opportunity to create this special bond. The first sexual encounter is unique in this regard.

The proper mental state is achieved when the *Nu-Matriarch* and *Nu-Patriarch* can keep their minds fixed on the seed during copulation when the energy of life is being transferred from one body to another. The awareness of this energy transfer is possible only when the mind is primed for procreation.

Because the purpose of the union is procreation, immediately after the seed is released parental anxiety is more intensified. This anxiety continues until conception is confirmed. When the conception is confirmed, the anxiety subsides and an attachment develops that inspires participation during the early stages of the child's development. The participation should include the cultivation of the mind.

The Flower of the Mind

God's third gift to the family is the mind. The mind is a field of ethereal elements that produce the flower of the intellect.

Like the body, Humarianism approaches the mind from an internal perspective. To develop the mind the ***Second Degree Humarian,*** in the role of the ***Nu-Patriarch*** and ***Nu-Matriarch,*** employs a process known as ***cultivating the intellect.***

Cultivating intellect is a procedure that prepares the mind to be educated. The ***Nu-Patriarch*** and ***Nu-Matriarch*** must assume the responsibility for implementing this procedure. It should begin immediately after the birth of the intellect, which usually occurs about twenty-six days after the embryo develops. Sound activates the conscious mind and awakens the intellect, which has the power to gather and store knowledge.

The first thought is a vision of the first sound, which acts as a trigger to vitalize the mental processes. Human life, before hearing the first sound, is akin to plant life; there is no active intellect. It is best described as the sensation of existence without any perception. Sound awakens perception, which initializes perceptual

Mind

reality. The quality of the first sound determines on what psychological level we begin our lives. Hearing is the first sense that comes into being. Brain function is initialized by hearing, as the brain, stimulated by sound, awakens the intellect.

Once the intellect is awakened, it should be kept engaged. The window for ensuring full development is the first three years of life. At no time during this period should the intellect be neglected.

The *Nu-Patriarch* and *Nu-Matriarch* should not wrongly associate the condition of the body with the condition of the mind. It is not uncommon to think that the mind of a newborn is inhibited by the physical limitation of its body. Forming a perception of the child predicated on what is perceived as physical inadequacies can have a detrimental impact on development. This misconception can lead to a presumption of ignorance, which can stifle the growth of the intellect.

The power of the intellect is not affected by the physical limitations of the body. The child's inability to speak the language has no affect on its ability to inquire. Inquiry can be made non-verbally. Intellectual potential is the same at birth as it is when the body reaches full maturity; what changes is the physical apparatus that allows expression. Children hear before they speak. They are given an opportunity to think about what they hear before they are given the ability to speak. A newborn has the same power of concentration as an adult. The parent's duty is to direct the focus.

Immediately after cerebral activation, that focus becomes sound. Sound plays a unique role in the development of the intellect. Humans have the highest

IQs because the sounds they communicate with have more content. What the human voice conveys separates humans from other forms of life. Using sound, humans can communicate more information than any other species.

Human beings are creatures of sound. Human consciousness can be elevated and lowered with sound vibration. In previous ages, the human voice could ignite fire, heal the body, unleash massive weapons of destruction, and even bring a body back to life. The human voice has properties that cannot be duplicated by any other form of life.

Of all the different species, the human is endowed with the broadest range of sound expression. The human voice can be manipulated to produce sounds that no other species can produce. Other life forms have greater limitations on their scope and ability to communicate with sound. Animals excel in areas of seeing, hearing, and smelling, but not in speaking. Dogs bark, pigs grunt, and birds sing. Their application of sound is limited by the variety of sounds they can produce and what they can communicate.

Animals use sound to identify one another, to respond to pain, for mating, to sound an alarm, and to locate a lost member. Animals cannot use sound for philosophical inquiry. Having the ability to inquire about God sets humans apart from other species.

It is through sound inquiry and response that humans develop intellect. Sound generates the objects of concentration. This exercise of mental calisthenics taxes the brain muscle and makes it stronger. Concentration is prompted by inquiry, the incessant desire to know. The intensity of this desire represents our mental appetite. A healthy body naturally craves food and drink, and a healthy mind naturally craves subject matter for contemplation. Sound provides that subject matter.

There are as many varieties of sounds as there are varieties of food, and all of them affect the mind differently. Sound can stimulate as well as desensitize. Spoken word communicates two ways: through word meaning and vocal intensity. Even though a child in the womb has no word comprehension skill, it can relate to pernicious sound. Sounds of hostility and rage disrupt mental functions and alter development. During early development, exposure to stressful sound should be minimized. The first sounds the child hears should be comforting, free of anxiety. When the conscious mind is activated by stressful sounds, the first response is fear, which unfortunately is often the first human emotion.

Hearing the first sound develops our sense and state of being. Even though we cannot comprehend what our existence is, we do sense an awareness of existence. Anything that threatens that existence causes fear. If the first sound heard in the womb is the mother crying, that sound accompanied by hostility can induce anxiety. If the mother's life is in jeopardy and she is being brutalized, her body will respond by secreting adrenalin and cortisol, stress chemicals that cross the placenta. Children who are exposed to these stress chemicals in the womb may be more prone to learning disabilities.

Before taking up the process of cultivating intellect, the Nu-Patriarch and Nu-Matriarch should learn as much as they can about how the mind and brain interact. The mind is a non-organic substance that emanates from consciousness. It exists outside the physical realm and therefore has no limit on perception or experience. It is the steering mechanism for the energy of life.

The innate molecules that compose the body and brain have no power to generate intelligence, which seems to indicate that the mind and the brain are two separate entities. The brain is the physical manifestation of the mind and, as such, has its own separate existence. The brain and the mind have no physical connection. The brain is a complex memory bank, transmitter, and receiver. The brain's knowledge is compiled from the body's responses to physical stimuli. It has no power to perceive that which exists beyond the purview and experience of the senses. Even though the brain has memory capability, it can only record the effects of physical stimuli.

Thoughts don't originate in the brain; they originate in the mind and provide direction to the brain, which is a response mechanism tuned to the mind's frequency. The mind directs the brain, which synthesizes thought into impulses that are relayed to the body for execution. The mind exercises control as long as its dictates are followed by the brain, which constantly switches from the transmit mode to the receive mode.

Thoughts enter the brain on two channels: one internal, one external. The most effective means of receiving and transmitting thought on the external channel is through sound vibrations. These sounds represent thoughts that originate in your mind and the minds of others. The external channel can also be used to receive and transmit thought visually and through touching.

Touch, sound, and visual thought transmissions are transmitted and received by the brain via the external channel. These thought transmissions are then transmitted to the mind via the internal channel. On the internal channel, only subtle thought vibrations in the form of dictates, inquiries, and responses are transmitted and received. Because there is no physical connection, the mind is not influenced by the physical stimulation of the body; the mind doesn't experience the body's pain; only the brain is affected.

The brain records the effects of physical stimuli on the body, which affects its conditioning. The mind's only contact with the body is through thought-directive transmissions received by the brain on the internal channel. The brain can't transmit and receive at the same time. When the external channel is being used, the internal channel is on standby. The mind may be dictating thought, while the brain is receiving dictates from the senses; because the brain can act on only one input at a time, the impulses from the senses often override the input of the mind.

The physical stimulation of the senses has more influence on the brain than thoughts transmitted by the mind. The brain caters to the dictates of the mind and the senses. You may be eating some high-fat food that is tasty and the mind tells you it's not healthy; but the taste is so powerful that the brain overrides the health concerns of the mind.

There is a constant struggle for control going on between the mind and the senses. The brain does not think; it only records the pleasant and unpleasant responses to stimuli. The brain and tongue can evaluate taste, but they cannot evaluate nutrition. This process requires the mind. The more you follow the dictates of the senses, the stronger they become, which weakens the influence of the mind. The mind's will is its strength, and its strength is increased when you follow its dictates.

A strong mind can exert its will over the senses and take complete control of your being. When the mind becomes weak, you are forced to rely on the brain. Developing a strong mind should begin in childhood, before the impulses of the body have a stronger resonance in the brain than thought transmissions from the mind.

The mind allows its greatest access during the first five years of life. After five years, access diminishes. There is no limit to how much knowledge the mind can absorb in the first five years of life. Focusing the mind of a child and keeping it engaged is how intellect is cultivated. The mind is energized by the urge to know, and the urge is greatest in the first five years of life.

The variance in intellect between different people also appears in the first five years of life. It may be attributed to the process used to cultivate the intellect. Controlling the sound environment is an effective way to stimulate the urge to learn. Sound vibration is the most dynamic form of thought transmission.

Early man did not read or write, neither did he use Braille or sign language. All knowledge was stored in his mind and was passed on through oral tradition. Sound is the most powerful medium of expression and as such has unlimited applications. It can be used to incite fear, anger, lust, envy, and greed. It can also be used to console, praise, and heal. Twenty-nine positive sounds are required to nullify the ill effects of one negative sound. This science works whether you are conscious of it or not.

How the sound environment is structured is a function of culture. To structure the sound environment, those who live for the black race use more negative sound vibration than positive. In this environment, children hear more negative comments by the age of five than positive ones, which limits expectations. The mind is conditioned to dismiss the positive and accentuate the negative. The cultural practice of creating a negative sound environment was introduced during slavery. The English language was purposely taught to slaves in a way to create negative sound space. It is one of the few vestiges of slavery that is still active today.

Slaves were talked down to by their masters and they adopted the same manner of speaking to converse with one another. Slaves were not taught to use language to affirm and compliment one another. Women talked down to men and men talked down to their children. The minds of the children were conditioned by the nuance of negativity.

Every concept must have an associated word to convey meaning. The term 'nigger' is a prime example of how negative sound space was created. To give meaning to the concept, a word had to be invented. If there is no word for it, the concept cannot be given life.

Sound creates perception, and negative sounds give life to negative perceptions. A negative sound cannot produce a positive perception, no matter how much affection you have for the term. This affection developed before the meaning of the term was clearly understood. The sound environment created by the use of the term 'nigger' is negative. The continuous use of the term sustains the perception. The reality of something is maintained by repeating the sound that represents it. The sound environment you create reflects your reality. This negative sound environment has been passed down from generation to generation. The effects today are the same as they were during slavery—low expectations and low self-esteem.

Nothing affects the development of the mind more than the sound environment it inhabits. It has been suggested that the first inquiry made by the mind after being awakened is, "To whom do I belong?" Our initial sense of existence is perceived as being part of something. Being connected is a source of comfort and security for the child, even if the something is negative. We become attached to the sound environment that we are first exposed to. If the environment is chaotic, that is what we will find ourselves drawn to.

Just as wholesome food is required to produce a healthy body, a wholesome sound environment is required to produce a healthy mind. The quality of the first sounds dictates what level of anxiety your life begins on.

As stated before, sound has numerous applications. It can be used to express love, joy, pleasure, sorrow, pain, and even hatred. If the first sounds a child hears in the womb are disturbing, such as its mother being brutalized, the child begins life in a high state of anxiety. This anxiety is generated by fear; fear of the space outside the womb. Your eagerness to learn is triggered by the first sound you hear. If the first sound you hear is the sound of suffering, how eager can you be to learn?

When the environment outside the womb is hostile and chaotic, cultivating the flower of the mind is made more difficult. Anxiety disrupts the learning process. To reduce this anxiety, the **Nu-Patriarch** and **Nu-Matriarch** should create a wonderful sound environment for their child. The sounds that the child hears outside the womb should be joyful and uplifting. They should paint a beautiful picture of the world inside the family circle.

Reading the family history, playing the family's favorite music, and speaking family affirmations allow the child to experience the sounds of the family. Repetition is very important in this regard. We are put at ease by things that we become familiar with. We develop familiarity through repetition. Hearing the same song or story over and over in the womb creates patterns of thought that trigger memory. What a child memorizes in the womb is not forgotten after birth. The same sounds that provided comfort in the womb are also found to be comforting after birth.

Comfort is found in order. Order creates the proper mood for learning. To invoke order, nothing is more effective than familiar sound. Sounds that were heard in the womb, such as the mother and father speaking, are the best tools for cultivating the flower of the intellect.

Cultivating the intellect is not about comprehension. The goal is to stimulate the desire to know. It's not about what the child knows; it's about how much the child wants to know. Creating an appetite for learning is important. This appetite cannot be created in a negative sound environment.

Negative sound does not inspire inquiry. Inquiry made in a negative sound environment is greeted with disdain, which stifles the appetite to learn. In this environment, the flower of the intellect only partially blooms. Children that hail from this environment are not as eager to learn. Their inquisitive nature is stunted. Once the flower has bloomed to your level of inquiry, your desire to know remains at that level throughout your life.

There is a three-year window for cultivating the flower of the intellect. To fully blossom, cultivation has to take place in a positive sound environment. Only in this environment can the desire to learn reach its peak. This environment should be created while the child is in the womb and it requires the participation of both parents.

The **Nu-Patriarch** and **Nu-Matriarch** that plan their conceptions bond with their children before they conceive them. At no time during the interim from pre-conception to birth should they loose contact with the seed. Twenty-six days after the embryo develops, the **Nu-Patriarch** and **Nu-Matriarch** should begin reciting the names of God.

The first sound that the child hears should be the name of God. No sound vibration can create a more positive sound environment. This sound vibration should be the first subject of inquiry. The cultivation of the intellect is perfected when the child's first inquiry is, "Who is God?" It was for that purpose that the family was created. The first institution to receive knowledge of God was the family, and in terms of knowledge the family's first responsibility is to deliver knowledge of God. When the inquiry is made, the child should not have to go outside the family circle to find the answer. This is the way of the Humarian.

11

Preserving Life Inside the Family Circle

There are millions of institutions in this world, but only one for which God personally chooses the members— the family. Man chooses to be a member of the church, temple, synagogue, and mosque, but no man chooses his birth family. The family is the oldest institution and the first to receive knowledge of God. It is the only institution that exists in both the spiritual and material world.

In America, this great institution has been lost to race. Family space, inside the circle, has been abandoned. Family members have been drawn outside the family circle by race. Living outside of the circle, the American people have been distracted by external prosperity. They owe this

prosperity to the race. The American people have become prosperous living for the race. They enjoy this prosperity outside of the family circle.

To bring members back into the circle, the family must offer what the race cannot. *Is there anything that the family can offer that the race cannot?* For those who have only known race as family, this question cannot be answered. For them, family and race are synonymous. The only people who can answer this question are those who live for the family.

People who live for the family, live in the garden. God has given every family a garden and in that garden He has placed the family tree of life. From that tree the family receives the gifts of body, mind, and spirit. Using resources that belong to the family, not the race, the family can become the most prosperous institution on earth.

The garden and its resources are what the family can offer that the race cannot. To offer the garden and its resources, the family must have them in their possession. They cannot offer something that has been lost to the race.

To realize its wealth, the family must control its resources; only then can the garden be cultivated. To take up this process, everyone must face inward so that they can see the condition of the family garden. Families who have always faced outward should not be surprised that the garden is full of weeds. Weeding must take place before anything can be planted.

The weeding process is reconciliation. To realize prosperity, the weeds in the family garden must be removed. To assist my family in the weeding process, there were four items of reconciliation that we addressed. The first item was to reconcile relationships with current family members.

Resolving Internal Conflict

To help my family resolve its internal conflict, I introduced the ritual of family forgiveness. Since the family was formed in the 1700s no attempt had been made to bring the family together to reconcile internal conflict. The family had been severely damaged by infidelity, child molestation, abortions, and out-of-wedlock births. Until recently there had been no instrument introduced that allowed family members to seek the forgiveness of the entire family. As a major contributor to the degradation of the family, I felt it incumbent on myself to provide such a vehicle.

The ritual of seeking family forgiveness dates back to ancient times. There are numerous ways to perform it. One way is to use the *Family Urn of Forgiveness.* If vested by the family the *Family Urn of Forgiveness* possesses enormous power. It can serve as a tool for family reconciliation. All families from time to time must engage in reconciliation and the Williams family is no exception. It's no secret that our family has weeds in the family garden. Some of these weeds are the size of large trees. There is a lot that has to be forgiven but until recently no attempt had been made to clear the overgrowth.

Every family has the power to grant forgiveness to its members. That power can be vested in the urn if sanctioned by the family. Using the urn, the family can atone for all of its misgivings. Anything you may have done to bring shame and dishonor on the family can be forgiven. The only thing required is a confession and a sincere plea for forgiveness, but forgiveness is not complete without the acknowledgement of wrongdoing.

To perform this ritual, our family confessions were presented in the form of letters. These letters, addressed to the family, were an acknowledgment of wrongdoing along with a sincere request for forgiveness. At the appointed time, each member put his or her letter in the urn. After all the letters were placed in the urn, the symbolic fire of forgiveness was lit. Fire has the power of purification. Consumed by the fire, what was contained in the letters was forgiven and never revisited. After performing this ritual, a tremendous burden was lifted from the family.

Since I initiated the process I was the first to place a letter confessing my shortcomings in the urn.

THE FAMILY URN
OF
FORGIVENESS

Letter of Confession

Dear Family,

I failed as a father, grandfather, brother, and son. As a son, I lived for the pleasure of my father. Winning his approval was the driving force in my life. Every path he took, I followed. No accomplishment meant more to me than winning my father's love. That love I never knew. Every attempt I made to earn it failed, I only succeeded in arousing his displeasure. The most disappointing moment of my life occurred when I was told at his bedside just before he died that he didn't want me there. I loved my father up to the moment he took his last breath but my love was not enough to secure his blessings. Out of frustration I did things that brought shame and dishonor to my family, things that I deeply regret today. I failed as a son and I also failed as a brother.

No brother could ask for three sisters who are more loving, compassionate, kind, generous, and supportive. My sisters are the personification of sweetness. They have been there for me day and night, rain or shine, hail and high water, but I have not been there for them. Instead, I fell victim to envy and jealousy. I resented my sisters because they were able to get what

I was always denied—my father's love and affection. They did something I could never do no matter how hard I tried—they were able to please my father. The pleasure he found in them became a source of pain for me. It was only after my father's death that I was able to overcome this. I failed as a brother and I failed as a father.

I have six wonderful children— Denice, Anthony, Fitzgerald, Charles, Christina, and Jodi, and I love them dearly. They know their father's love and I try to support them in all of their endeavors. This, however, has not always been the case. The first five years of life are the most critical. What a father can contribute to the life of his children in the first five years cannot be estimated. It was in this area that I failed my children. I did not provide the academic support, the creative influence, the discipline, and the moral support they needed. There is nothing a father can do to recapture those precious years if they are lost. I lost those years with all of my children. Even though they know that I love and support them today, there is nothing I can do to atone for my neglect during the most critical phase of their development. I failed as a father and I also failed as a grandfather.

I have ten wonderful grandchildren and four great-grandchildren and in the past none of them have gotten the quality time from me that they deserve. I have not been there on special occasion such as birthdays and graduations. I have not been in the stands during sporting events or at their bedside during illness.

These words have not come easy. One of my biggest problems in life has always been my unwillingness to admit failure. Yes, I have failed my family and I'm sorry. I would like to take this opportunity to ask each and every one of you to forgive me. My gift to you is a promise that for the rest of my life I will try to be the best father, grandfather, son, brother, uncle, cousin, and nephew that I can possibly be. To do this I need your help and most importantly I need the help of God.

Tucker Family Olive Hill Cemetery

"Reconciling the Family's Relationship with God"

The family is God's creation. We belong to a family before we belong to any other institution. This is how God arranged it. Family is very dear to God. What we do for Him as a family is more pleasing than anything we do in any other institution. The family belongs to God. He created it. To fulfill its purpose the family must recognize His sovereignty. One way to accomplish this is to prepare a place for God in the center of the family and ask Him to take His place and lead the family home. We approach God as individuals, but we should also approach God as a family. When we do so we reconcile the family's relationship with God.

To honor my grandfather, the family formed the family circle around his grave and prayed the family prayer for deliverance.

Williams Family Gathering

Reconciling the Family's Relationship with the Descendants of the Slave Owner

To provide my family with a deeper historical perspective, I traced my family history back to the time when the Williams name was transferred to the family. On June 18, 2005 the Williams family—one black and one white—gathered once again on Panther Creek Plantation in Lewisville, NC, the place where the families first made contact in the late 1700s. This time they came together not as master and slave but as people of goodwill who had a desire to put the past behind them. The purpose of the gathering was reconciliation. Joseph Lanier Williams, the grandson of Nicholas Lanier Williams, the man who owned my great-grandfather, Henry Williams, spoke the following words.

Plea for Reconciliation

"First let me welcome all of you to Panther Creek Plantation. This is indeed an historic occasion. Like I told Charles Williams, I never thought that any slave descendant would ever come back to Panther Creek. When he showed up at my doorstep, I was thoroughly amazed. Slavery was, and is, an evil institution, and yes my family owned slaves. The slaves at Panther Creek, however, were not thought to be slaves; they were servants. And as servants they were treated with dignity and respect. This is by no means an excuse for slavery. No matter how humanely you treat your slaves, slavery is and will always be an evil institution. Today we come together not as master and slave, but as people of goodwill who wish to put the past behind us, and as a token of my desire to do so I would like to offer you a gift. Let this boxwood tree symbolize the future hopes and aspirations of both of our families. Let us walk away from this place, hand in hand, sharing a vision of making the Williams name as great as it can be. I thank all of you for coming, and God bless you!"

Lanier Williams

Someone might ask how can you reconcile the horrors of slavery? How can you excuse such gross inhumanity? "Nothing can justify the enslavement of another human being. Those who did so were wrong." Hearing these words spoken sincerely from the heart followed by the offering of a token gift of reconciliation was appropriate, I think, for someone seeking forgiveness for the past transgressions of his ancestors.

The acceptance of the gift and the granting of forgiveness in response completed a critical step in the reconciliation process. Success in this endeavor gave us the momentum we needed to take another critical step, which was to reconcile our relationship with our enslaved ancestors. Most families lack the information required to engage in this process. When a typical family peers back into the past, they only see darkness; there is so much that has not been brought to light.

Reconciling the Family's Relationship with Its Enslaved Ancestors

Within this great chasm of darkness the identities of our enslaved ancestors have been lost. This has done great harm to the relationship between the ancestors who were enslaved and their descendants. Out of frustration, many of us have abandoned our relationships with our ancestors and to our detriment have lost their favor. However, not knowing their identity has not severed the connection. Even though we may not know them, it is in our best interest to honor the sacrifices they made.

Panther Creek Plantation, Lewisville, N.C.

If we fail to honor those who paid the ultimate price, the legacy we leave for our descendants will be empty. To honor the sacrifice made by our ancestors the family conducted a memorial ceremony in their honor. A monument was erected, their names were recited, and a tree was planted in their memory.

After removing the weeds through reconciliation the family can began the cultivation of the garden.

12

Planting the Seeds of Family Identity

Tending the family garden was the first occupation given to man. Drawn out by race, man has abandoned the garden. The space inside the family circle is not being cultivated. To cultivate this space, the seeds of family identity must be sown. The following items are potential seeds of family identity. The family must give form to them. Planting these seeds in the family garden, the family will reap a bountiful harvest.

FAMILY HISTORY SEED

1. FAMILY BIOGRAPHY

The family's most valuable asset is its history. The family story is the literary foundation on which the family is built. Every family member past, present, and future has his or her own chapter and verse in the family book of life. No vehicle has more power to unify the family. Compiling its biography is a task that every family should undertake.

2. FAMILY GENEALOGY

A complete genealogy and family tree should be generated for publication in the Family Biography. Each family member should have a copy of the Family Genealogy and proudly display it in his home.

3. FAMILY HISTORIAN

The duty of the historian is to gather, file, and preserve for posterity all of the historical records of the family. These records may be in the form of letters, photographs, copies of deeds, wills, estate records, birth, death and marriage certificates, newspaper clippings, obituaries, wedding announcements, military papers, taped interviews, community awards, commendations, degrees and work histories, to name a few.

FAMILY LEADERSHIP SEED

1. FAMILY LEADERSHIP

Organizing the extended family is no different than organizing any other group of people— you begin by selecting leaders. The leadership should be chosen through an electoral process. Depending on which leadership structure the family chooses, leadership council, president, secretary, treasurer, board of directors, or some other format, a nominating process and election should be held to choose the family leaders.

2. EMPOWERING THE LEADERSHIP

The Family Leadership Council should be given the authority to draw up the Family Charter, the document that governs the family. The Family Charter should contain the family mission and vision statement, and the family bylaws.

3. LEADERSHIP RESPONSIBILITES

The leaders should be responsible for organizing events such as family reunions, family retreats, and business meetings. Leaders should also be responsible for incorporating the family and establishing and managing the Family Trust Fund. Other responsibilities include the establishment of a family resource database, family Web site, and drawing of the Family Charter.

THE FAMILY CHARTER

Article 1
FAMILY LEADERSHIP COUNCIL

This charter authorizes the establishment of the Family Leadership Council. This body selected by the family is vested with the power to represent the family's interest in all matters.

Article 2
DECLARATION OF SOVEREIGNTY

On this day _____ , we the members of the Family Leadership Council, exercising the power vested in this body by the family, duly recognize from this day forth the sovereignty of the Williams family. As a sovereign entity, the family assumes responsibility for all of its members. By decree, each member is authorized to represent the family. To represent the family properly, members must put the interest of the family ahead of their own personal ambition. Only then can the sovereignty of the family be maintained.

Article 3
FAMILY CENSUS

By decree of the Family Leadership Council a family census will be taken every two years.

Article 4
INCORPORATION

By decree of the Family Leadership Council the family will be incorporated as a non-profit organization.

FAMILY OPERATIONS SEED

1. FAMILY TRUST FUND

One of the chief functions of the family leadership will be to establish and manage the Family Trust Fund. Each adult family member should be invited to contribute to the trust fund. Trust funds offer families numerous tax benefits and also protect valuable family assets from government seizure. These funds can be invested on behalf of the family and the profits used for scholarships, college tuition, family emergencies, and the administrative cost of running the family organization.

2. FAMILY RESOURCE DATABASE

To help the family harness its full potential, a Resource Data Base should be compiled and made available to family members. The database should contain the resumes of all the adult family members. This information will allow the family to take full advantage of the knowledge, talent, professional experience, and resources the family has to offer. The database should be maintained and operated by the Family Secretary. The duty of the secretary will be to maintain files on all the family members, record the minutes at family meetings, and act as a liaison for the family reunion.

3. FAMILY WEB SITE/E-GROUP

To maintain a sense of unity the family needs a place to gather and communicate on an ongoing basis. The Family Web Site/E-Group will make this possible The Web site should be updated on a regular basis and the E-Group would provide access to the latest family news and information about upcoming family events.

FAMILY FORMATION SEED

1. FORMATION PLAN

The formation plan is a structural document that explains how the family will be formed. In this document the family makes known what the accepted procedure is for expanding the family. An example is:

ARTICLE ONE

"In the Williams family, sex before marriage is forbidden."

ARTICLE TWO

"Conceptions in the marriage should be planned and announced to the family beforehand so that a conceptual rite can be performed."

ARTICLE THREE

"At birth all children should have a birth rite performed."

The formation plan should also contain a Family Pledge. Once recited the pledge authorizes members to act as representatives of the family.

Sample Pledge

I _____, solemnly pledge to do everything in my power to represent my family with dignity, courage, love, integrity, and respect. As a representative of the _____ family, I dedicate my life to the future success of this institution. From this day forth, let it be known that my first responsibility is to my family.

FAMILY SIGNATURE SEED

1. FAMILY SYMBOLS

The family signature is the symbol that is chosen to represent it. Symbols such as a family crest or seal are given life when they visually depict traditions that are honored by the family. Family identity is born of shared traditions, and symbols that depict these traditions help keep the traditions alive. For instance, if the family tradition is that the family plants a particular tree every time someone in the family dies, the tree should be incorporated into the family seal or crest. If the family has a tradition of kissing babies feet, that should be visually depicted.

2. FAMILY CUSTOMS

One of the biggest challenges we face today is how to take our families back from the race. The family has become the race. Family competes with race for sovereignty. When the family becomes the race, the family loses its individuality. It cannot regulate itself because it has no life of its own. The family is sacrificed to maintain the identity of the race. To take the family back from the race, customs must be established that restore the family's identity. These customs should serve as guardrails to guide the family from within.

HEALTH AND WELLNESS SEED

1. COMPILE FAMILY HEALTH HISTORY

A family medical history or medical family tree is a record of illnesses of family members. It resembles the family tree with the addition of health information. A medical family tree visually depicts the relationships between each member of your family. Depending on how much information you're able to obtain for each relative, your medical family tree can be very detailed and include health issues that each family member has faced.

2. PREVENTIVE HEALTH PROGRAM

To keep the family abreast of the latest innovations in the field of health and wellness, a nutritionist and physical therapist should be invited to attend large family gatherings such as family reunions. These professionals should conduct seminars on the latest techniques being employed in the area of diet management and exercise. Advice should be offered to family members to help improve their overall health and increase their longevity.

FAMILY TRADITIONS SEED

1. FAMILY RITUALS

Family rituals such as Rites of Passage Ceremonies prepare young people for adulthood and instill a deeper sense and appreciation of family. Honoring the transition from youth to manhood and womanhood is a wonderful tradition that all families should embrace.

2. FAMILY TRADITIONS

To strengthen the family, traditions are essential. It's important that each family adopt traditions that represent their values and ideals. One tradition that might be helpful is the family day of worship once a month. On this day, such as the first Saturday of the month, regardless of where family members are at a designated time, the entire extended family should engage in some form of praise and worship. Reading from scripture, fasting, prayer, or whatever the family decides is appropriate should be done on that day.

3. COMMUNITY SERVICE

The family is the foundation of human civilization and should be involved in community development. Volunteering to help feed the homeless, care for the aged, assisting the handicapped, and any other volunteer work should be encouraged.

Planting these seeds and nurturing them, the family can come to know itself as God intended, beyond race. There is life beyond race. The best place to live this life is Humaria, the place inside the family circle. With God in the center, no family has to rely on race for its identity.

13

In Summary

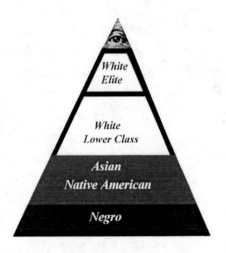

"Living in the House of the Races"

All human beings have the power to create space, external as well as internal. The space I refer to here is consciousness. In its unadulterated state, consciousness is transparent. It has no color; neither does it have any form. Within this space we build our institutions. Those who have built external institutions have done so for personal gain. Class is a prime example.

Class is one of the oldest external institutions established. Class consciousness was erected to impose domination. To house this institution two spaces were required—one for the upper class and one for the lower class. These two states of consciousness cannot exist in the same space. The consciousness that imposes domination is not the same as the consciousness that submits to domination. For class to be instituted, both states of consciousness were required.

To erect the *"House of the Races"* the same principle was applied. The first United States Census created the space that was used to build this institution. Of the three documents, the Census, the Constitution, and the Bill of Rights, the Census has proven to be the most powerful because it created white and black space. Prior to 1790, no government had ever produced a founding document that divided it citizenry according to race.

The white space created by this document is extensively America's crown jewel. Protecting the jewel has become a way of life. It was taken up immediately after the first census was answered. In response to census data, quarters were built to house all of those who participated. Space in the house was allocated to each party according to their race. To ensure that there was ample accommodation, the *"House of the Races"* contained four floors. The top floors were configured to accommodate those who lived in whiteness, the middle floor for others, and the bottom floor for those who lived in blackness.

The first Americans to don the cloak of whiteness were the firstborn of British aristocracy. The initial assimilation of whiteness took place amongst the elite between 1680 and 1700. In its first incarnation, whiteness was hoarded by the sons of privilege. It was not shared with the working class.

British immigrants who entered the nation as common laborers could not sit at the table of white privilege. The men who sat at this table were from the ruling class. Although power was the main attraction, the appeal of whiteness was also bolstered by weak family identity.

In the new world, it was very difficult to maintain family ties with relatives back on the British mainland. Only a small percentage of those born to privilege in America went back to Britain to connect with extended family. What the sons of privilege in America came to know as family was not connected to the family root. The past generations, who were steeped in family tradition, had little or no influence on their American brethren. The flavor of the British family was not transferred to America. With no connection to its British root, the American family was left open to racial exploitation.

The Assimilation of Whiteness

At its core, whiteness is a rebuke of family. Whiteness competes with family for the sovereignty of its members. To eclipse the family, whiteness offered something that the family could not—ascendancy. This position was far beyond the family's reach. There is no history of any American family that came together to wage a campaign to secure racial domination. This power was sought after and acquired by a cabal of conspirators who were not blood relatives. The construction of whiteness took place outside the family circle. The catalyst behind this endeavor was the acquisition of individual power.

The collaborators who constructed whiteness did so to enhance their standing as individuals, not to elevate the family. The individual derives the greatest benefit from whiteness, but at the same time whiteness limits the expression of individuality. There is always a danger of having whiteness revoked. Failing to protect white space can result in the loss of white privilege. This is especially true for a female. A black male in the arms of a white female is considered a breech of white space. Allowing such a breech to occur, the female can lose her privileges.

A black female in the arms of a white male is not considered a breech, which appears to be somewhat of a double standard. Although the white male has greater latitude for individual expression, he too must contend with limitations. No white male can father a white child with a black woman. The white race will not allow him. In essence, whiteness perverts individual expression. No family connection is needed to express your whiteness as an individual; all you need is race. When you live in whiteness you have no incentive to be family. The race gives a voice to the individual that the family cannot. Speaking for the family does not equate to speaking for the race. Thomas Jefferson and his cohorts spoke for the race. Speaking for the race, they constructed white space. This was done outside the family circle.

There are two ways to form the family circle. One way is for members to face inward. Facing inward the family can claim the space inside the family circle. The other way to form the circle is for members to face outward.

Facing outward, the sovereignty of the family can be lost. Its sovereignty is lost when it fails to claim the space inside the family circle. To identify with race, the member must be facing outward. Facing outward, you cannot claim the space inside the family circle. Race is space created outside the family circle. When the family claims this space, its sovereignty is lost to race. With its sovereignty lost, the family lives for the pleasure of the race. Living for the race, the family has to maintain the integrity of white space. To do this, the family allows race to dictate family behavior.

In the space that whiteness creates, race gives life to the family. To reside in white space, the family must carry out the dictates of the race. The construction of blackness was the first dictate. Nothing gives more life to whiteness than blackness. To realize ascendancy, whiteness and blackness must be housed in the same quarters.

Whiteness was assimilated in Britain long before the New World was colonized, but to realize ascendancy whiteness had to be flaunted in the presence of blackness. This was not possible in Britain as the demographics would not allow it. There was not enough blackness to warrant the construction of a *"House of the Races."* In Britain, without someone to lord over, British whiteness was an exercise in futility. In places like Scotland, Wales, and Ireland, the fangs could be shown but there was no blackness to devour.

This was not true, however, in America. American whiteness, unlike British whiteness, had numerous subjects to plunder. There has always been blackness in one form or another for American whiteness to lord over, so much so as to warrant the construction of the first *"House of the Races."* Before building this massive structure, the population was prepared by the architects for residency. Of major concern was security. Out of fear of insurrection, the laboring class was partitioned according to race. Laws were passed by the elites to draw a clear distinction between blackness and whiteness.

To recruit the security force, immigrants from amongst the common stock were offered a place at the table of white privilege. For providing security to protect the interests of the elite, members of the laboring class were extended privileges. The acceptance of white privilege created the racial divide needed to secure white space. With white space secure, black space could be created; this was done, by imposing blackness.

The Assimilation of Blackness

In its original form, blackness only existed as space. The people who were forced to occupy the space did not identify with blackness. They did not identify with anything outside the tribal circle. The Ibo, Ashanti, and Fulani, lived their lives inside the circle where there was no blackness. The only blackness that existed was outside the tribal circle.

Blackness and whiteness are external constructs. The architects of whiteness also constructed blackness. Like whiteness, blackness was constructed outside the family circle. Although forced to occupy black space, the Ibo, Ashanti, and Fulani, refused to turn outward to embrace the chimera of blackness. They never ventured outside the tribal family circle.

Whiteness

Blackness

Blackness was not, constructed by the people held captive in the space; it was constructed by those who submitted to the dictates of the white race. They decided who would be bound in shackles and chains, denied an education, not allowed to marry and form a traditional family, work and not get paid. Unlike white space, the people in black space did not own or control their own space. They were forced to assimilate an identity that was dictated by whiteness.

Rape, murder, kidnapping, and castration, could not persuade those who were born in the land of Ibo, Ashanti, and Fulani to give up the tribal circle. Even while held captive in the black space of America, they never let go of their ancestral roots.

The first proponents of Negro identity were born in the Americas. The assimilation of this alien identity took place in the shadows outside the tribal circle. To break up the tribe, the family was broken. The people were forced to breed without establishing family ties. The object was to produce free labor. To be identified with a family, a person must know whom he or she is related to. The family is a reality only when the members can be identified. Those who controlled black space made this difficult to do.

Like their white counterparts, the Negro had no contact with family back in Africa. The family that was known in America consisted of a mother and siblings. In most instances, the biological father was not present. If the father was present, the family population was still very small. The first generation of Negroes had no extended family in America.

No records have ever been found of any African family that was imported to America and maintained intact. Destroying any semblance of a family line was a tactic used by the architects of whiteness to impose blackness. With the family circle broken, slaves were forced to go outside the family to find an identity. For those who were born in black space, the identity that they assimilated was blackness.

The assimilation of blackness by those who occupied black space completed the last phase of construction. The first *"House of the Races"* was built and was being occupied by the early 1800s. Since the house was completed, there has been only one major renovation. The renovation took place in the 1960s. After 250 years, the people at the bottom finally took control of black space. After forty-eight years in control, they have produced a President, a Supreme Court Justice, Secretary of State, National Security Adviser, Cabinet Members, CEOs of major corporations, stardom, fancy clothes, cars, mansions, yachts, and a per capita income that surpasses any third world country. What the people have failed to do, however, is to change the position of the space.

Nothing done in blackness can change its position in the *"House of the Races."* The people may have control of the space, but they did not create it. It was created for them by an adversary. The space is attached to the house and the house was built to impose domination.

In the *"House of the Races,"* blackness must live at the bottom; whiteness dictates it. For those who live at the bottom, there is no future. The only hope is to withdraw from the space. To withdraw from the space you must let go of blackness. Blackness and the space are one; the two cannot be separated.

Instead of holding onto space that holds you captive, new space should be created. The best place to create this space is in the family garden. In this place you find the family tree of life. From this tree the family receives the gifts of body, mind, and spirit. These gifts were given to the family, not the race. To gain entry into the *"House of the Races,"* the family has to give up its gifts. When you look into the mirror in the *"House of the Races,"* the image you see does not belong to you, it belongs to the race. Everything belongs to the race, your body, your mind, and your spirit. Living in the *"House of the Races,"* you own nothing. You pay the ultimate price for the use of alien space and identity.

In this alien environment, you will not find the center of the family. The space created by race denies access to the family circle. You live your life in the *"House of the Races"* facing outward. To find the center, you must face inward. Facing inward you can escape the *"House of the Races."* To face inward, you must let go of blackness and whiteness. If everyone lets go of his race, the *"House of the Races"* would collapse and the world would be a much better place.

Life Outside in the Garden

Your life has been compiled into a book. Everything you have done in this life has been recorded. At the time of death, your book of life will be read to you. What will the title of your book be? Will the title be *"Living in the House of the Races"?* If this is indeed the title, your book will not have a happy ending. Everything done in the *"House of the Races"* is for naught. Living for the race is not living for God, no matter how you try to package it. Nothing you do in the *"House of the Races"* pleases God.

God has no race, but God does have family. Pleasing God is about pleasing the family. To please the family, you must tend the family garden. God has given every family a garden to work. Living in the house, the family cannot tend the garden. To tend the garden, the family must leave the house. Leaving the house, the family will discover that the garden is overgrown. To clear the overgrowth, the family must take up the process of reconciliation.

To reconcile, the first task undertaken should be to prepare a place for God in the garden. An ideal place is where your beloved ancestors have been laid to rest. In this place, the family should form the family circle and say a prayer asking God to come and take His place in the center, and henceforth, this place should be viewed as a holy place of pilgrimage. Everything brought into the family garden should be brought here first. It should be shared with those who preceded you. With God residing in the garden, all the seeds that the family plants will be blessed.

Even though you may be in the last chapter of your book, it is not too late to change the title. The question is, *can you let go of Race?* Can you let go of Whiteness, can you let go of Blackness. The answer is *yes.* Everyone can let go of race. You can change the title of your book. A great title would be *"Living in the Family Garden."*

The process of letting go has been laid out in this book. Everything required to resolve the race issue is found here. There are those, however, who will dismiss this book as just another attempt to tear down the nation. They will point to all the positive things that the nation has done in the world while ignoring all the negative things they do to preserve their whiteness.

To preserve whiteness, you must live in white space. White space is above blackness. To live above blackness, America constructed the *"House of the Races."* The *"House of the Races"* is a prison house. The people who live in whiteness are prison guards and those who live in blackness are the prisoners. The guard's duty is to ensure that none of the prisoners escapes blackness. To keep them confined, the guards put the prisoners in a box. Everyone is in a box in the *"House of the Races,"* including the guards. The black boxes are at the bottom and the white boxes are on top.

WHITE BOX

BLACK BOX

The white boxes are for the guards and the black boxes are for the prisoners. The prisoners committed the crime. The crime was taking birth. The color of their skin convicted them.

America can be greater than this. To realize its true greatness, the *"House of the Races"* must be dismantled. If dismantling this prison house is what the naysayers view as tearing down the nation, so be it.

Charles Williams

Living for the Race

Looking in the mirror
And what do I see?
I see an image that
Don't belong to me

I paid too much
For this identity
My body, mind, and soul
From now to eternity

Somebody tell me
Somebody tell me please
What can I do, to
Restore my humanity

Chorus:
I'm living in White Space
I'm living for the White Race
I'm living in Black Space
I'm living for the Black Race

Living, living, living, living
Living, living, living for the Race

Everyone living, living in this space
Everything you do, you do it for the race
Everything you think and everything you say
Everything you feel and every prayer you pray

You do it for the race
You do it for the race

Somebody help me get out of this place
Take me somewhere that there is no race

Everything I think, everything I say
I do it for the Race
I do it for the Race

I got race in my blood
I got race in my bones
Race in my heart
And Race in soul

Living in White Space
Living for the White Race
Living in Black Space
Living for the Black Race

Living, living, living, living
Living, living, living for the Race

Charles Williams

BIBLIOGRAPHY

Akbar, Na'im. The Creation of the Negro [online] 2004. mindpro.com/documents

Allen, Theodore W. The Invention of the White Race. London: Verso, 1994.

Berlin, Ira. Generations of Captivity A History of African-American Slaves. Cambridge: Harvard University Press, 2003.

Boles, John B., Ed. Masters and Slaves in the House of the Lord: Race and Religion in the American South 1740–1870. Lexington: University Press of Kentucky, 1990.

Bonnett, Alastair. "Constructions of Whiteness in European and American Anti-Racism," Rodolfo D. Torres, Louis F. Miron, Jonathan Xavier Inda, eds. Race, Identity and Citizenship Reader. New York: Blackwell Publishing, 1999.

Broughton, Viv. Black Gospel: An Illustrated History of the Gospel. London: Sterling Publishing Co., 1985.

Caldwell, Rev. H. "Slavery and Southern Methodism: Two Sermons Preached in the Methodist Church in Newman, Georgia. [online] 1865. www.archive.org

Clegg II, Legrand H. Ebonics: A Serious Analysis of African American Speech Patterns [online] 1997. www.melanet.com/clegg_series/maat.html

Curry, Walter Clyde. The Middle English Ideal of Personal Beauty. Baltimore: J. H. Furst Co. 1916.

Davis, James F. Who Is Black? One Nation's Definition. University Park: Pennsylvania State University Press, 1991.

DuBois, W. E. B. "The Talented Tenth," The Negro Problem: A Series of Articles by Representative Negroes of To-Day. [online] 1903. www.yale.edu/glc/archive/1148.htm

Emerson, Michael O. & Christian Smith. <u>Divided By Faith:</u> <u>Evangelical Religion and the Problem of Race in America</u>. Oxford: Oxford University Press, 2001.

Finkelman, Paul. "Jefferson and Slavery: Treason Against The Hopes of The World" Onuf, Peter, ed. <u>Jeffersonian Legacies</u> ed. Charlottesville: University Press of Virginia, 1993.

Fox-Genovese, Elizabeth & Genovese, Eugene D., <u>The Mind of</u> <u>the Master Class: History and Faith in the Southern Slave Holders</u> <u>Worldview</u>, New York: Cambridge University Press, 2005.

Garvey, Marcus. <u>Marcus Garvey and the Universal Negro Improve-</u> <u>ment Association, Vol X</u> Los Angeles: University of California Press, 2006.

Gershon, Rabbi Stuart W. Those Who Get To The Promised Land Are Those Who Overcome Their Fears [online] 2008. www.templesinainj. org/content/sermons/pdf/2008-06-20-Sermon.pdf

Glaude, Eddie S. <u>Exodus!: Religion, Race and Nation in Early</u> <u>Nineteenth Century Black America</u>. Chicago: University of Chicago Press, 2000.

Goad, Jim. <u>The Redneck Manifesto</u>, New York: Simon & Schuster, 1998.

Guglielmo, Jennifer & Salerno, Salvatore, ed. <u>How Race Is Made In</u> <u>America: Are Italians White?</u> New York: Routledge, 2003.

Hakim, Ida, Ed. <u>The Debtors Whites Respond to the Call for Black</u> <u>Reparations,</u> Caucasians United for Reparations and Emancipation (CURE), 2005.

Hakluyt, Richard. <u>The Principal Navigations, Voyages, Traffiques and</u> <u>Discoveries of the English Nation.</u> New York: MacMillan Co., 1906.

Harris, Cheryl. "Whiteness as Property" <u>Harvard Law Review</u> [online] 1993. http:/www.scholar.google

Hodes, Martha Elizabeth. <u>White Women, Black Men: Illicit Sex in the</u> <u>Nineteenth-Century South</u>. New Haven:Yale University Press, 1999.

Hodgson, John. History of Northumberland [online] (1840) www. archive.org

Heuman, Gad J. & Walvin, James. The Slavery Reader. New York: Routledge, 2003.

Hurmence, Belinda, Ed. My Folks Don't Want Me To Talk About Slavery. John F. Blair, 1984.

Isaacs, Harold. The American Negro and Africa: Some Notes. The Phylon Quarterly, [online] 1959. www.jstor.org/pss/273045

Jefferson, Thomas. Notes on the State of Virginia.1853 [online] http// etext.virginia.edu/toc/modeng/public/JefVirgi.html

Jordan, Winthrop D. White Over Black: American Attitudes Toward the Negro 1550-1812. Chapel Hill: University of North Carolina Press, 1968.

Kemper, Charles. "The Calhoun Ancestry" [online] www.jstor.org/ pss/1921317

Kidd, Colin. The Forging of the Races Race and Scripture in the Protestant Atlantic World 1600–2000. Cambridge: Cambridge University Press, 2006.

Ku Klux Klan, La Porte, Indiana Charter, [online] indianahistory.org.library/manuscripts/collection_guides/om0352. html

Loewen, James W. Lies Across America: What Our Historic Sites Get Wrong. New York: Touchstone, 2000.

Lovell, John. Black Song: The Forge and the Flame The Story of How the Afro-American Spiritual Was Hammered Out. New York: Macmillan, 1972.

Malone, Dumas. Jefferson and His Time. Charlottesville: University of Virginia Press, 2005.

MacLeod, Duncan. Slavery, Race and the American Revolution. Cambridge: Cambridge University Press, 2008.

Middleton IV, Richard. "The Historical Legal Construction of Black Racial Identity of Mixed Black and White Individuals: The Role of State Legislatures" [online] 2007. papers.ssrn.com

Morrison, Michael & Stewart, James Brewer. Race and the Early Republic: Racial Consciousness and Nation Building in the Early Republic. Landham: Rowman & Littlefield, 2002.

Muhammad, Elijah, Message to the Black Man in America, Chicago: Secretarius Memps Publications 2006.

Nesbit, Robert. Prejudices: A Philosophical Dictionary. Cambridge: Harvard University Press, 1982.

Plato, The Last Days of the Socrates, New York: Penguin 1995.

Roediger, David R. "The Pursuit of Whiteness: Property, Terror and Expansion 1790–1860" Morrison, Michael & Stewart, James Brewer, ed. Race and the Early Republic: Racial Consciousness and Nation Building the Early Republic, Landham: Rowman & Littlefield, 2002.

Roy, William G. Making Societies: The Historical Construction of Our World, Boston: SAGE Publications, 2001.

Schneider, Dorothy & Carl J. Schneider. An Eyewitness History: Slavery in America From Colonial Times To The Civil War. New York: Checkmark Books, 2001.

Schwartz, Marie Jenkins. Born in Bondage. Cambridge: Harvard University Press, 2001.

Schwartz, Robert. "Race is a Poor Measure", New England Journal of Medicine, vol. 344 No. 18 (2001).

Scobie, Edward. Black Britannia: A History of Blacks in Britain. Chicago: Johnson Publishing Company, Inc., 1972.

Silberman, Charles E. Crisis in Black and White. New York: Random House, 1964.

Singleton, Theresa A. I, Too, Am America. Charlottesville: University of Virginia Press, 1999.

Smith, David Jr. The African American Presidents: The Founding Fathers of Liberia, 1848–1904. New African American History Press, 2004.

Snowden, Frank M. Jr. Before Color Prejudice: The Ancient View of Blacks. Cambridge:Harvard University Press, 1983.

Talty, Stephan. Mulatto America: At The Crossroads of Black and White Culture. New York: Harper Collins, 2003.

Thomas, Hugh. The Slave Trade: The Story of the Atlantic Slave Trade 1440-1870. New York: Touchstone, 1997.

Warry, John Gibson. Warfare in the Classical World. Baltimore: Salamander Books Ltd., 1980.

WGBH/PBS, "Africans in America: America's Journey Through Slavery" 1998.

Williams, Charles. Restoring Black Humanity. Atlanta: Parenting Institute of America, 1999.

Wood, Peter H. Black Majority: Negroes in Colonial South Carolina From 1670 Through the Stono Rebellion. New York: W. W. Norton & Company, 1974.

Index

269